Caribbean Cookbook
A Lifetime of Recipes
Written by Rita G. Springer

Rita G Springer

2

Caribbean Cookbook
A Lifetime of Recipes
Written by Rita G. Springer

Edited and produced - Sally Miller
Photography - Andrew Hulsmeier, Video & Photo
Images
Design - Eightzeronine Design Associates Inc.
Food Styling - Sally Miller & Neil Barnard
Pre-press input - Roma Cozier, Lyn Armstrong

Published by Wordsmith International

Distributed by Miller Publishing Co. Ltd.
Edgehill, St. Thomas, Barbados, West Indies
Tel: (246) 421-6700; Fax: (246) 421-6707
E-mail: miller@caribsurf.com

ISBN   976 9515 32 9
        978 976 9515 32 1

Printed in Singapore

4

I dedicate this book to my
twin great-grandchildren
Maia Gabrielle and Joshua Alexander Springer
Born in Trinidad & Tobago on 05/05/05
Now residing with their parents in
Dubai, United Arab Emirates

Contents

7	Foreword
9	The First Cookbook
10-11	Introduction
12-15	Measures, Temperatures & Cooking Tips
14	Traditional Caribbean Cooking Equipment
17-21	Herbs, Condiments, Dressings & Seasonings
23-27	Soups
29-41	Fish
43-53	Meat Dishes
54-55	One-dish Meals
57-63	Milk, Egg & Cheese Cookery
65-69	Energy Foods
71-79	Salad & Vegetables
81-93	Popular Desserts
95-107	Coffee & Tea Occasions
109-113	Preserves & Candies
115-125	Cooling Thirst Quenchers & Cocktail Eats
127-143	Traditional Dishes of The Caribbean
129	Jamaica
131-133	Barbados
135	Trinidad & Tobago
137	Guyana
139-141	Asian Heritage
143	European Heritage
145	Using Leftovers
148-150	Common Cookery Terms
151-154	Glossary
155-160	Index

Foreword

Rita Springer is a culinary icon in the Caribbean. Her original Caribbean Cookbook, first published in 1968, is a paperback classic and continues to be widely used and sold throughout the Caribbean and beyond by Ian Randle Publishers.

Rita is a delightful individual and this new edition's elegant format, with her recipes accompanied by high quality photographs for the very first time, is a fitting tribute to her lifetime's work.

Rita Springer's comprehensive repertoire of West Indian recipes is simply written, using a wide variety of fresh ingredients to make tasty, wholesome food for everyday living and entertaining in Caribbean style. The contents also offer a wealth of practical information about food and nutrition, which is helpful to all those involved in culinary pursuits.

As a bonus, Rita has included some amusing anecdotes and retrospectives about her life in the Caribbean over the last 93 years!

As she would say, Bon Apetit!

Sally Miller

The First Cookbook

My first attempt at writing a cookbook was in 1956 when I was teaching at the House Craft Centre. It was about the same time that Roberts Manufacturing Company introduced their margarine products to the local market. I was invited by the Manager and Board of the Company, through a mutual friend, to undertake to introduce their new product to the local housewives and others in the market. They asked me to organize the procedures.

I suggested that the best way might be to give the information in clubs, schools and institutions, and so with the help of the Social Welfare Officer, I made a list and contacted about 60 groups via a circular, to arrange a meeting and convenient times when I could inform them about the products and introduce them into their kitchens via a demonstration and fireside talk.

Dates and times were arranged with these people. After a few weeks the Company arranged transport for me to travel throughout the island four evenings a week, after working and school hours, from say about 4.30 on, to deliver these talks and demonstrations.

At the end of 3 months I accomplished this mission, and we saw that most Barbadians had by now heard of margarine products, Glowspread, Mellocream and VelvoKris for cake making and general household use, especially cakes and pastries. The management was well satisfied with the progress made in the local market and they asked me to compile a small booklet of about 80 recipes which were used regularly in houses. This I did and produced "Recipes for the Islands", a copy of which was given afterwards to customers buying their local

Charles and Rita Springer at Buckingham Palace in 1962

products. Many friends tell me that they still use that first copy of the cookbook I compiled. The management has used it and improved on it over the years and I understand that it is still available. The products are certainly still used in the community.

Since the early part of the last century, say since the first World War, there has been a revolution in food preparation, and very old customs started to change in Barbados and the larger Caribbean islands.

I remember growing up in the 1930s, that the standard of living was very low. Wages were generally low because those in the lower economic groups, living in small wooden cottages and chattel houses, used to work on the plantations or kept small shops in the country and city areas. The meals were composed generally of cheap starchy foods that were cheap items. Fish were cheap, and sheep, goats, pigs and chickens reared at home were the protein foods.

Tin smiths did a good trade in those days because many kitchen utensils were made of tin, imported in sheets from Europe, and sold in the large hardware stores. Cups, bowls, measurers, graters, plates, pans for baking were all made out of tin. The potteries in St. Andrew also produced clay coal pots, three legged pots and Dutch pots, jugs, bowls etc. A water jug with a spout in which to keep drinking water cool, known as a "monkey", was commonly seen in houses then, and even up to today.

Only the middle income and upper class people could afford to buy the imported crockery and other household items imported from Europe and North America by the business houses. About this time in the Caribbean there was emigration to the USA and this brought a change in the plight of the poorest people. Those who worked in the USA sent back home money and goods to their families. This helped the standard of living to rise.

Political changes in the island were also helpful. Again in the 1950s there was migration to the U.K., and with political influence, standards rose again and the poorer classes were able to improve their standard of living. Cheap household goods were also available from the East and houses became better furnished.

Tourism was beginning to develop and workers at home were able to get more lucrative jobs and tourists demanded foods they were accustomed to at home. With hotel standards going up and training in improved methods of food preparation being offered by government, people in all income groups introduced them in their homes and everyone wanted to provide healthy and tasty foods for their families, hence the vast improvement in cooking methods and the desire for good kitchen equipment and utensils.

Today, saucepans are available in stainless steel and even copper if you desire them. Beautiful cutlery, crockery and glassware in all shapes and colours are available to meet what one can afford. Linen is available in great variety to enhance your table. You can make your choices.

Householders graduated from the fire hearth and coal pots in clay and iron, to consolidated wood burning cast iron stoves using wood blocks, to oil stoves and gas and electric stoves of high quality and what we see today.

During the same period improved cooking methods were taught and used, as well as the nutrition involved, and the good presentation of food which is now at a very high level. Despite the fact that all groups of people eat outside the home today and fast food seems to have taken over, the majority of people still prefer a well prepared home-cooked meal for their families.

In those days the only instruction in Domestic Science was the Girls Industrial Union, a private institution run by a board of local ladies. It was situated on Constitution Road in a cottage next door (east) of the present Ministry of Education, opposite Queen's Park.

It was opened in 1912 and offered classes for girls from all income groups for training in a number of household skills and they were taught by some members of the board and school teachers and the students did very well.

The Girls Industrial Union is still open today, housed in Pine Road with fewer pupils but still doing good work. Some of the well known ladies who managed the classes were Mrs. Olga Symmonds, Miss Gladys Williams, the Leslie sisters - Miss Claudine Leslie and Mrs. Meta Williams - Mrs. Gladys Cummins, Mrs. Edna Bishop and many others. These ladies have now all passed on but Mrs. Olga Symmonds' daughter, Dame Patricia Symmonds, is now patron of the organization.

I joined the Girls Industrial Union before I left school and learnt much of the skills I acquired at that institution. I sewed for myself and family, cooked for them and also did many years in catering at home and abroad. My mother, a good cook and seamstress, taught me all she knew, although my father did not like to see me in the kitchen. He thought I would get in the way of the cook. My mother intervened and gave me chores to do that I could manage and taught me baking and pastry making and some sewing.

In the 1950s after I was married, I was appointed to be a visiting lecturer at the House Craft Centre, a government institution, and was able to pass on some of my cooking skills there. In the 1950s the House Craft Centre was situated in Lower Bay Street. It was merged with the Community College in the 1960s and the School, now a Hotel School, is housed at the Pom Marine Hotel in Marine Gardens, where pupils of both sexes can do courses in Hotel Management.

In the UK in 1964 I took a two year course at the Royal Society of Health. When I graduated and was granted associate membership of the Royal Society of Health I had already done the script for the Caribbean Cookbook and I was allowed to take the exam only in Nutrition and complete the course in one year instead of two.

I was fortunate to have attended both these institutions for they have taught me much in home cooking and other skills.

Rita at the launch of Caribbean Cookbook in 1968 which is still sold in paperback throughout the Caribbean and beyond by Ian Randle Publishers.

Standard Measures

Three standards for weights and measures are generally used - Metric, British Standard Imperial and American or Canadian Standard. All quantities given in this book are based on the American standard, but for reference the British Standard Imperial is also quoted here.

The British Standard measuring cup holds 300ml (1/2 pint). The American Standard cup is 8 fluid ounces, half the American pint which is 16 fluid ounces.

Liquid Measures

Quantity	Metric	British Standard Imperial	American or Canadian Standard
3 teaspoons	1 tablespoon	1 tablespoon	1 tablespoon
2 tablespoons	30ml	1/4 gill	1/8 cup
4 tablespoons	60ml	1/2 gill	1/4 cup
8 tablespoons	150ml	1 gill (1/4 pint Imperial)	1/2 cup
12 tablespoons	225ml	1 1/2 gills	3/4 cup
16 tablespoons	300ml	2 gills (1/2 pint Imperial)	1 cup
1/2 pint	300ml	10 fluid ounces (1/2 pint)	8 fluid ounces
2 cups	600ml	20 fluid ounces (1 pint)	16 fluid ounces (1 pint)
4 cups	1.2 litres	1 quart (Imperial)	1 quart

Measuring various foods

All recipes in this book will make 4-6 servings, except where otherwise stated. For successful results, it is essential that all measuring is done accurately. All measurements given are level. Use standard 8oz measuring cups (American) in glass or plastic, preferably one for liquids and another for dry ingredients. A set of measuring spoons in plastic or aluminium is also required.

Dry ingredients
Fill the measuring cup or spoon to overflowing and level off with a knife edge. A rounded spoonful is as much over the top of the spoon as there is in the spoon.

Liquids

Stand the measuring cup on a level surface and measure carefully.

Syrup

Syrup or molasses leaves the cup or spoon more readily if the measures are greased or wetted with cold water.

Sugar

Roll out any lumps before measuring brown sugar and sift granulated, castor and icing sugar.

Shortening

This may be butter, margarine, lard or a mixture of these. To measure 1/2 cup of shortening, fill a measuring cup 1/2 full of water and put in shortening until it reaches the cup level. Shortening may easily be cut in quantities required, bearing in mind that 100g = 1/4 lb = 1/2 cup.

Oil or melted fat

Dip measuring spoon in fat and be sure to lift it out quite full.

Equivalent measures

450g (1lb) bananas	3-4 cups
450g (1lb) fine breadcrumbs	4 cups
450g (1lb) butter	2 cups
450g (1lb) grated cheese	4 cups
1 square plain chocolate	1/4 cup (grated)
450g (1lb) cocoa	4 cups
1 coconut (grated)	4 cups
450g (1lb) cornmeal	3 cups
12-14 egg yolks	1 cup
8-10 egg whites	1 cup
25g (1oz) powdered gelatine	2 tablespoons
450g (1lb) lard	2 cups
450g (1lb) margarine/butter	2 cups
450g (1lb) minced meat (raw)	2 cups (packed)
450g (1lb) molasses (cane syrup)	1 1/3 cups
1 medium onion (chopped)	1/3 cup
450g (1lb) rice	2 cups
Rind of 1 orange (grated)	1-2 teaspoons
Rind of 1 lime (grated)	1/2-1 teaspoon
450g (1lb) dried peas or beans	2 cups
450g (1lb) raisins/currants	3 cups
450g (1lb) peanuts (shelled)	3 cups
450g (1lb) brown sugar	3 cups
450g (1lb) granulated/castor sugar	2 cups
450g (1lb) icing sugar	3 1/2-4 cups
450g (1lb) large tomatoes	4-5 medium

Oven temperatures

Oven settings vary according to different makes and sizes of ovens, therefore the following temperatures may not indicate precisely the conditions in individual ovens. However, they will act as a basic guide.

Gas Thermostat	Temperature of Oven	Oven Heat
1/4-2	130-150°C/250-300°F	Very slow
2-4	150-180°C/300-350°F	Slow
4-6	180-200°C/350-400°F	Moderate
6-8	200-230°C/400-450°F	Hot
8-9	230-240°C/450-475°F	Very hot

Traditional Caribbean Cooking Equipment
(Excerpt from "Caribbean Cookbook" by Rita G. Springer first published in 1968)

Old cookery methods are still commonly used in the area as certain types of equipment have been handed down from generation to generation.

1.   The smokeless fireplace consists of hearth stone in concrete with a firebox at one end, in which a wood fire is made, and a flue at the other end, to draw out the smoke. Cooking is done on top of the heated stone. This is used in many rural areas.

2.   The Caledonian stove is a large, old-fashioned cast iron range. Wood or coals are used in the firebox. A flue at the back draws out the smoke and allows the fire to burn. The heat is controlled by a damper. It has a built-in oven and 4 to 6 burners.

3.   Coalpots in cast iron and clay are still used in both urban and rural areas. Fuel costs are low when compared with oil, gas or electricity and often the latter facilities are not available.
From tradition and custom, iron coalpots are still used in modern and well-equipped homes, for cooking pepperpot, stews and dishes which require long hours of simmering. Fuel costs are thus reduced.

4.   In many rural areas, the box oven is the only type of oven used. This is made from a wooden crate lined with zinc or tin, fitted with wire shelves, and heated by a coalpot set on the floor of the box. With a little patience and skill, these ovens work very satisfactorily.

5.   The dutch pot (buck, stewing pot) is a shallow (3-4 inch deep) flat bottomed, cast iron pot, generally used on any type of stove, or over coals on a trivet on a coalpot, for stewing, frying or pot-roasting.

6.   The three-legged iron pot (dutch pot) is very deep, standing on legs which rest on the coals or on a trivet over a coalpot.

7.   The cast iron saucepan, with a tin cover and long handle at one side, is used on any type of stove, as well as over a coalpot.

8.   The yabba pot made in glazed clay to withstand great heat is also very familiar in rural areas. Glazed mixing bowls in clay are still popular. Large jars for storing, water coolers, water jugs, canarees or casseroles, are other articles in clay.

9.   The tawa is a flat iron griddle 10-12 inches in diameter, used for baking cassava bread, roti, scones, bakes, etc.

The very large mortar and pestle is seen in many homes where pounded plantain (foo-foo) is regularly made.

Baking Tips

1. Set the oven to the required temperature about 10 minutes before the dish under preparation is finished, so as to allow time for the temperature to be reached before the start of baking. A small counter top oven requires less pre-heating.

2. The setting on a thermostat registers the temperature in the centre of the oven. The top will be hotter, the bottom cooler unless it is a fan assisted oven.

3. Bake small cakes and pastry at the top of the oven, large cakes in the centre and rich fruit cakes on a lower shelf.

4. When baking rich fruit cakes and gingerbread, grease and line the pans with two thicknesses of greaseproof paper, to prevent mixture from burning.

5. Test large cakes by inserting a knife or skewer in the centre. If it comes out clean the cake is finished.

6. Dishes of custards should be put in a pan of boiling water while baking to maintain an even, slow temperature which allows mixture to set gradually otherwise it may curdle. Custard is finished when a knife inserted in the centre comes out clean. Test pumpkin pie in the same way.

7. Avoid opening the oven until after the first 1/2 hour, especially when baking sponge cakes and light batter mixture.

8. When roasting chickens or large joints of meat, cover with aluminium foil until the last 15-20 minutes of baking. Then raise the oven temperature, and allow the meat to brown. The use of foil precludes the necessity for basting.

9. When using a meat thermometer, be sure that it is pushed into the thickest part of the meat. The thermometer should not touch the bone.

10. If baking on more than one oven shelf at the same time, avoid crowding of pans. Space must be allowed for circulation of hot air for the best result.

Herbs, Condiments, Dressings & Seasonings

The success and popularity of Caribbean cookery are undoubtedly due to the subtle ways in which the foods are seasoned and garnished with herbs, spices and condiments to suit the various types of food. Everyday and simple dishes may thus be made more enjoyable and flavourful. There is a very wide variety from which to choose, and personal tastes and experience prompt the correct choices.

The most popular seasonings used for meats, fish, stews, soups, poultry dressings and savoury dishes are: onion, salt, chives or eschalots, thyme, sweet marjoram, parsley, celery, garlic, bay leaves, etc. These are generally used fresh or green. Dried pepper powders are commonly used, especially when hot fresh peppers are scarce, such as paprika (dried sweet pepper), cayenne and chilli powder (from red pepper), and black and white pepper. Cloves, curry powder, garlic and celery salts are also popular. Soy sauce, cassareep, tomato ketchup, mustard, and Worcester sauce add flavour to certain dishes. Cinnamon, nutmeg, mace, ginger, lime or orange rinds are chiefly used in sweet dishes, such as desserts, puddings, bread and cakes.

A bouquet garni is used in flavouring stews and soups. It consists of sprigs of thyme, sweet marjoram, a bay leaf, chives or eschalots, celery or a similar mixture of herbs as desired.

A Basic Marinade for Meats

To season pieces of meat or poultry for stewing, and liver, chops etc., they should be marinated for about an hour, to soak up the blended flavourings. To marinate two to three pounds of meat, mix together the following:

1 tablespoon salt or less
2 teaspoons sugar
2 tablespoons malt vinegar
1 medium onion (sliced)
2 tablespoons cooking sherry or rum
1 teaspoon paprika or
1 teaspoon chilli or black pepper
1/2 teaspoon celery salt
1/2 teaspoon garlic salt or
1 large clove garlic (chopped)
1 tablespoon soy sauce (for chicken)

This mixture is rubbed well into the meat and allowed to stand for the required period. After browning the meat, the residue of the marinade with the sliced onion is added with water for cooking and making gravy. Alternatively, the meat pieces may be shaken out of the marinade, dredged in seasoned flour and fried. The residue of marinade, with a little brown colouring and butter added, may be heated, thickened with a little flour, and used as a separate gravy.

Fish fillets, steaks and small fish may be marinated similarly, using lime or lemon juice in preference to vinegar, omitting the sugar, and using less salt for the same amount of fish.

Seasoned Flour

This is used for dredging all kinds of meat, fish, etc. before frying. Mix together:

1 cup flour
1 tablespoon sugar
1 teaspoon salt
1 teaspoon paprika
1 teaspoon white or black pepper
1/2 teaspoon powdered cloves
1/2 cup breadcrumbs

Combine this mixture well, store it in a glass jar until ready for use.

19

Mango Chutney ingredients

Mango Chutney

4 cups under-ripe mangoes (diced)
1 cup raisins
1 cup dates
100g (4oz) green ginger
1 teaspoon mustard seed
4 cups sugar
50g (2oz) salt
2 cloves garlic
2 hot peppers
4 cups malt vinegar
225g (1/2lb) onions

Cut up dried fruit and peppers (a food processor may be used for this); add to vinegar and allow to steep until the next day. Prepare diced mangoes, add sugar, peeled and finely chopped ginger, garlic, chopped onions and other seasonings. Boil all ingredients together over a very low heat until chutney is thick and brown. Stir periodically to ensure that it does not catch on the bottom and burn. Follow the instructions for bottling in the Preserves and Candies section.

Seasoning Mixture

1 medium onion
2-3 blades chives (eschalots)
piece of red hot pepper
1/4 teaspoon powdered cloves
1 teaspoon salt
sprig of thyme or marjoram
1 clove garlic
1 teaspoon lime juice

Peel and chop onion very finely, also green seasonings and garlic. Mix in the other ingredients and chop in a blender or food processor. Score the flesh deeply in places and put a little mixture in each incision. Fish fillet pieces, flying fish and pork for roasting may be made very tasty, prepared with this seasoning mixture. This method of seasoning is typically Barbadian style.

French Dressing

For marinating vegetables, a French dressing is desirable, and each type of vegetable should be treated separately before arranging them in a salad.
A simple French dressing is as follows:

1 teaspoon salt
2 teaspoons sugar
1/4 teaspoon white pepper
1/4 cup vinegar (white) or lime juice
1 teaspoon salad oil (optional)
1 teaspoon grated onion

Shake well before using.

Soups

There are many advantages in serving soups:
1. Scraps of vegetables, meat and bones may be used up instead of being thrown away, thus avoiding wastage.
2. All the flavour and food value of the ingredients are retained as the liquid in which they are cooked is the main part of the dish.
3. Time and fuel are saved by cooking in one pot.

Thick hearty soups are very popular as main dishes or even complete meals. These comprise root and green vegetables, green or dried peas, added to any available fresh or salted meat, bones, salt or fresh fish, or even peanuts. Grated cheese, milk or cream may be added to soups after cooking to give extra nourishment.
Thin soups, purées and broths are served as first courses of more formal meals, to young children and during illness and convalescence. Stock for soup (with pieces of meat, bones and vegetables) is usually freshly made, other ingredients being added as desired, thus the keeping of a stockpot is not customary in the Caribbean area.

Garnishes and accompaniments for soups
Thin soups and broths are served with crisp biscuits, toast and dumplings as desired.

Purées or sieved soups are improved when garnished with grated cheese, a blob of fresh cream, chopped parsley or croutons.

Thick soups, like stews, rarely need extra accompaniments as they are flavourful and filled with pieces of meat, vegetables and dumplings.

For creamed soups, cups of white sauce may be blended with the ingredients in the particular recipe and chopped parsley or shredded cheese used for garnishing.

Pumpkin Soup

Pumpkin Soup

450g (1lb) pumpkin, peeled and cut
2 onions
1/2 cup split peas (soaked
beforehand)
pepper and salt to taste
225g (1/2lb) salt meat and bones
2 green outer cabbage leaves (cut
finely)
piece of thyme
1 tablespoon butter

Slice and lightly fry onions in
butter. Add the rest of ingredients.
Cover with water and simmer for
about 1 hour. Blend before serving.

Fish Soup

450g (1 lb) deboned fish
6 cups water
2 or 3 English potatoes
1 tablespoon butter
1 medium onion
1 tablespoon tomato ketchup
2 blades eschalot
sprig of marjoram
salt and pepper to taste
1 tablespoon lime or vinegar

Wash and clean the fish with lime
and salt. Put all ingredients in
saucepan to simmer for about 2
hours. Crush potatoes and add
butter and lime juice just before
serving.

Rabbit or Chicken Soup

900g-1.35kg (2-3lb) rabbit or
chicken
6 cups water
thyme and sweet marjoram
1 tablespoon vinegar
2 or 3 cloves
1 dessertspoon Worcestershire sauce
450g (1lb) potatoes
2 onions
salt and pepper to taste
1 clove garlic (crushed)
1 teaspoon sugar

Wash and cut up the meat. Put it
into a saucepan with water and
simmer until tender. Add
seasonings and boiled crushed
potatoes. Just before serving, stir in 1
dessertspoon Worcestershire sauce.

Chilled Cucumber Soup

3 tablespoons flour
1/2 teaspoon paprika
1 chicken bouillon cube or a tin of
chicken broth
1 tablespoon lemon juice or 1
teaspoon of lime juice
1 1/2 teaspoons salt
3 cups milk (or half milk, half cream)
1 tablespoon grated onion
1/4 teaspoon red pepper sauce
3 cups shredded cucumber
1 teaspoon sherry
green food colouring (optional)

Sprinkle flour and seasoning over
the milk and mix thoroughtly. Place
over a saucepan of boiling water,
add bouillon or stock and onion.
Stir constantly until the soup
thickens - about 10-15 minutes.
Remove from heat and stir in the
lemon juice, cucumber, a teaspoon
of sherry and some green colouring
(optional). Blend and chill
thoroughly. Stir well before serving
and if liked a little chopped parsley
can be put on the top of each
serving.

Breadfruit Soup

1 medium sized ripe breadfruit
8 cups of water
100g (1/4lb) salt meat (previously soaked)
bunch of herbs
100 g (1/4lb) fresh meat
1/2 teaspoon pepper
1 large onion
salt to taste

Boil peeled and sliced breadfruit in water with meat, cut in pieces. When tender, crush smoothly or puree with a hand blender and return to saucepan with remainder of ingredients. Stir occasionally and simmer for 1 hour. Strain through a colander before serving with pieces of meat.

Eddoe Soup

Replace the breadfruit above with 900g (2 lbs) eddoes.

Peel eddoes, cut in pieces and put in water to boil with salt and fresh meat also cut in small pieces. Crush eddoes when cooked using a hand blender or placing them in a blender. Add seasonings. Simmer and add 1 dessertspoon of parsley just before serving.

Split Pea Soup

2 1/4 cups split peas (green or yellow)
1 ham bone or 225g (1/2lb) salt meat
2 large sliced onions
1 teaspoon salt or salt to taste
piece of fresh hot pepper or
1/2 teaspoon pepper
225g (1/2lb) pumpkin or carrots
bunch of mixed herbs

Cover peas with 5 cups of cold water and soak overnight. Add ham bone or salt meat, onion and seasonings. Bring to boil, cover, reduce heat and simmer for 1 1/2 hours. Stir occasionally. Remove bone; cut up meat. Return meat to soup and add vegetables. Cook slowly, uncovered, for 30 to 40 minutes. Add salt, blend and serve.

Skirt Soup

450g (1 lb) goose neck
225g (1/2 lb) pigtail or salt beef
6 cups water
8 green bananas (cooked & crushed)
onion, chive, thyme,
whole green pepper

Boil meat in water till tender. Cut into pieces, Add cooked and crushed green bananas and seasoning to taste, and simmer until soup is of a thick consistency. Remove pepper before serving.

Mutton Soup

675g (1 1/2lb) mutton neck or bones
salt and pepper to taste
5 cups water
few blades chives (eschalots)
50g (2oz) rice
1 sprig parsley
100g (1/4lb) carrots or turnips
1 bay leaf
1 large onion (chopped)

Chop bones and cut off meat, discarding fat and skin. Put into saucepan with water, add onion and seasonings and simmer for 1 hour. Strain, then add the rice and diced vegetables with the pieces of meat and cook until tender. Serve hot.

Chicken Broth

1 old fowl
1 tablespoon vinegar or lime juice
1 chopped onion
6 cups water
1 teaspoon chopped parsley
1 oz rice
salt and pepper to taste

Cut meat from the fowl and chop this and the bones into small pieces. Simmer in the water and vinegar, onion, salt and pepper for at least 2 hours. Add rice and, when tender, serve sprinkled with parsley. This broth spoils quickly in the warm climate so keep well chilled.

Callaloo Soup

4 bunches eddoe/dasheen leaves
675g (1 1/2lb) fresh meat
100g (1/4lb) shrimps
225g (1/2lb) salt meat
1 sliced onion
450g (1lb) ground provisions
(yams, potatoes, cassava, etc.)
salt to taste
few blades chives and thyme

Cut up salt meat, soak for 1 hour and put to boil with fresh meat. Cut up leaves with seasonings and add to meat after 1 hour's boiling. Add prepared shrimps, vegetables and simmer until tender. Salt to taste. Dumplings may be added.

Okra Soup

1 dozen okras
1 small bunch callaloo
salt and pepper
225g (1/2) lb salt beef
4 cups water
seasoning (tomatoes, escallion, thyme, piece red hot pepper)

Wash salt beef and soak overnight. Cut up the okras, and put them in water along with beef, and simmer gently for 2 hours. Add finely chopped callaloo. Simmer. Add seasonings. The soup may be blended before serving

Dumplings for Soup or Stew

1 1/2 cups flour or
1 cup flour plus 1/2 cup cornmeal
1/2 teaspoon salt
1/2 cup water or milk
2 tablespoons sugar
1 dessertspoon margarine or butter
1 teaspoon baking powder
pinch of powdered mixed spice or nutmeg

Mix dry ingredients together. Rub in fat and add liquid to make a soft dough. Drop by spoonfuls in soup and cook for 10 minutes.

Mixed Vegetable Soup

1 1/2 cups diced vegetables (carrot, christophene, cauliflower, broccoli, celery, pigeon peas)
1 sliced onion
1 cup water
2 tablespoons butter
1 cup milk
salt and pepper

Cook vegetables in melted butter for about 3 minutes, stirring constantly. Add water, cover and cook vegetables until tender (about 15 minutes) Slowly stir in milk. Reheat and serve.

Beef Soup with Vegetables

675g (1 1/2lb) beef
6 cups water
1 cup tomato juice
1 large onion (chopped)
1 dessertspoon salt
1 teaspoon Worcestershire sauce
1 tablespoon oil or fat
small piece fresh hot pepper
1 bay leaf
100g (1/4lb) diced carrots
1 cup chopped cabbage or chocho
bunch of mixed herbs
225g (1/2lb) yam or sweet potato (sliced)

Remove meat from bone and sauté in hot fat. Add bones, water, tomato juice, onions and seasonings. Cover and simmer for 2 hours. Add vegetables cover and simmer for another hour. Remove bones and bay leaf before serving.

Fish

The Caribbean Sea and the Atlantic Ocean to the north and east abound in fish of many varieties available all the year round. There are two kinds of fish:

1.   The oily or fatty fish with dark flesh which include species such as the jack, cavalli, tuna or bonito, herring, mullet, salmon, etc.
2.   The popular white fish with lean flesh usually in large varieties, like the dolphin, king and red snapper, bream, barracuda, flying fish, grouper, shark, etc.

Fish is as nutritious as meat, both being animal protein. It has less fat and contains more water than the same weight of meat. It is easily digestible and the white varieties, especially, may be served to young and old. The rich source of gelatine in fish may be preserved by using the stock from steamed and boiled fish as gravy with the addition of butter and seasonings.

When buying fish, be on the lookout for certain characteristics. Select those with bright eyes, colour and red gills, having firm flesh with the scales well fixed. They should have a fishy smell without a strong odour. Bear in mind that fish varies greatly in price according to the state of the market, therefore the price of fish is no indication of its quality or nutritional value. The cheaper varieties of fish are often a much better buy than the more popular and usually larger ones, so flexibility in choice may be an advantage.

Flying fish frequent clear warm waters in many parts of the world and have often been seen from ship decks, leaping in and out of the water. In the Caribbean, Barbados is known as the Land of the Flying Fish, where there are large catches between December and June. These fish are delicious when boned, well seasoned and steamed or fried in fillets. Many of Barbados' souvenirs are made or carved in the shape of the flying fish.

There are many flavourful ways of cooking fish. The small oily fish are generally fried, broiled or steamed. The larger fish may be boiled, fried in steaks, stuffed, baked, curried or stewed. Using either method, cooking time should be relatively short. Overcooking causes fish to dry, become tough, break up and the flavour is also destroyed. The flesh should be flaky when finished. Salt, lime or lemon juice or vinegar is always used in the preparation of fish and, for serving, lime or lemon slices.

Shellfish

Shell fish is plentiful in many areas. Like salt water fish, it is rich in minerals, especially phosphorus and iodine, but it is coarser in texture and not as digestible.
1. The crustaceans, i.e. lobsters, cray fish and crabs, which frequent the clear reef waters. Black or land crabs live in swampy areas. Shrimps are harvested mainly from the banks around the northern coast of South America, and in lesser quantities in other areas.
2. The molluscs, i.e. oysters, small and large clams.
Sea eggs are a popular delicacy in Barbados. They are the roes of a sea animal which lives in a round prickly shell. The sea egg season is around September and October when the roes are mature. Some years harvesting is outlawed in order to protect the sea egg population. Tinned fish, locally processed or imported, such as salmon and sardines are very nutritious and useful when fresh fish is scarce or unavailable. This provides extra calcium as the bones are eaten in this processed state. Fish may be dried successfully and although some of the flavour is lost, the protein and mineral values are, however, increased.

Salted cod fish

Salted cod fish or salt fish, as it is commonly known, was imported from the early days of slavery by the colonists, and used as the main protein food for their slaves and domestic servants. Since trade between Canada and the Caribbean started early in the last century, salted cod fish has been imported almost exclusively from that country up to the present day. There was much snobbery regarding salt fish before the Second World War, but as food became scarce and salt fish became more and more expensive, it was gradually accepted by all income groups as a worthwhile protein substitute. Salt fish dishes are today very tastily made and widely used. Small well-seasoned fish balls made from it have long been popular cocktail snacks. Salt fish and ackee is Jamaica's most popular national dish.

Before preparation, salt fish must be washed well and soaked in cold water for several hours or overnight if necessary. The salt solution is discarded. It may be boiled up quickly and the water drained off, but the latter method reduces the flavour. The fish is then flaked or pounded and seasoned and mixed with other ingredients to make the required dishes.

Preparation of fish

Cleaning: Rinse fish to remove any sand slime. Lay it on some rough kitchen paper and scale on both sides with a dull-edged knife. Rinse off the scales. Slit the belly from just below the head to halfway down the body. Remove and discard the entrails preserving any roes or melts. The head of some fish, e.g. snapper, may be left on. In this case, remove the gills; otherwise, cut off the head around its base, also the tail. Rinse the fish well with lime juice, salt and water.

Steaking: To remove the back fin, make an incision with a sharp knife along each side of it, and from the tail end pull it firmly out. Remove the small fins likewise. The fish is now cut across in about 2.5cm (1in) round steaks.

Filleting: The whole piece of fish from below the head to the tail is called a fillet. Fillets may be cut in pieces, i.e. fillet steaks. To cut the fillets, use a sharp knife and split the fish down the centre back to the bone. Working from the head downwards, cut the flesh cleanly all the way to the tail by keeping the knife pressed down to the bones. Remove the fillet on the other side similarly. The bones and head may be used for making soup stock.

To skin the fillets, lay them on a board with the skin side down. Holding the end of the tail skin firmly in the left hand, and using a sharp knife in the right hand, make a sawing motion between the flesh and skin of the fish from the tail end upwards pulling the skin firmly with the left hand until it is separated from the flesh.

Boiled fish

Fish is allowed to steam rather than boil, and large whole fish or large fish steaks are suitable, e.g. whole red fish, dolphin (dorado) or king fish steaks (crosswise cuts). Clean the fish and marinate it in lime and salt. Place in enough boiling water to make the gravy required, add salt, pepper, sliced onion, butter and a little mixed mustard to taste. A few small garden tomatoes or tomato ketchup may also be added. Simmer together until the fish is easily removed from the bone. Serve with slices of lime.

A small quantity of fish may be seasoned similarly and steamed in a soup plate placed over a saucepan in which other food is being cooked. Cover the soup plate with the saucepan lid or plate, steam the fish, turning it once during cooking, for 20-25 minutes, or until it is finished.

Fried fish

Fish must be dried before frying and coated to prevent fat from soaking into it. Steaks and thick slices of fish should be fried in shallow fat as they require thorough cooking. Rissoles, croquettes, etc., including cooked fish are coated with batter and fried in deep fat for quick cooking. A deep saucepan with a frying basket is used. The basket should be heated in the fat before the food is fried in it, so as to maintain the temperature of the fat.

Fillets, steaks and small whole fish are best for frying. Marinate fish as for steaming. A little seasoning paste may be rubbed over the fish, if desired. Dredge the fish steaks, etc., in seasoned flour (p19). Allow steaks to stand a little, then fry in hot fat until brown. Alternatively, the fish may be dipped in beaten egg, dredged in breadcrumbs and flour, and fried. Serve with slices of lime or lemon and parsley.

Grilled fish

Steaks, cutlets, fillets, and small whole fish may all be satisfactorily grilled. Dry the fish, season it, brush with melted butter and score the flesh of whole fish to avoid the fish drying outside before it is finished cooking. Grease the grill rack to prevent fish from sticking to it. Cook for a short period turning fish from one side to the other. Time: about 7-15 minutes.

The Dolphin misunderstanding

The delicious fish referred to as Dolphin that is caught and eaten throughout the Caribbean in large quanities is a scaly fish that is also known as Dorado or Mahi Mahi. It is often mistakenly thought, by visitors to the region, to be the mammal Porpoise, which is also referred to as Dolphin. Those Dolphin are never eaten in the Caribbean.

Fish Pie

Fish Pie

450g (1lb) white fish
2 cups milk
3 tablespoons butter for sauce
2 tablespoons flour
thyme, parsley, salt, pepper
1/2 cup white wine (optional)
50g (2oz.) grated cheese
450g (1lb) potatoes or yam
chopped parsley
2 large tomatoes
1 minced onion
breadcrumbs
2 tablespoons butter for assembling
pepper and salt to taste

Poach fish for a few minutes in milk, salt, pepper, seasoning, herbs and a little white wine (if using). To cook the sauce, melt butter in saucepan over low heat. Blend in flour. Add poaching liquid all at once. Cook, stirring constantly with a wooden spoon until the mixture thickens. Cook for 2 minutes. Shred fish and arrange half in greased baking dish, sprinkle with chopped parsley, pepper, salt, onion, grated cheese and a little lime. Add a layer of sliced vegetables and a layer of tomatoes. Dot with butter. Repeat layers, top with vegetables, cover with cream sauce sprinkled with breadcrumbs and dot with butter. Bake in a moderate oven for 15-20 minutes. Garnish with parsley.

Baked Stuffed Fish

1 whole fish (1.35kg or 3lb white fish, preferably)
1 tablespoon seasoning mixture
1 cup bread or biscuit crumbs
1 onion (chopped)
salt and pepper to taste
1 tablespoon chopped herbs
1 clove garlic (minced)
2 tablespoons butter
2 tablespoons chopped pickles
water to moisten

Clean fish well, leaving on the head. Rub in a little seasoning mixture and stuff with the other ingredients mixed together to moist consistency. Skewer or sew the cut side of the fish. Baste with butter. Place it in a buttered baking dish with a cup of hot water. Bake in a moderate oven for about 3/4 hour. To make gravy, add sliced onion and a little brown colouring to cooking water 20 minutes before it is finished.

Fish & Vegetable Mould

675g (1 1/2lb) any fish
celery or cucumber
1/4 cup chopped olives or pickles
1/2 cup French dressing (p21)
1 cup chopped carrots
salt and pepper
5 cups fish stock
piece of red sweet pepper
1 large onion
3 tablespoons gelatine

Soak gelatine in cold water. Cook fish, onion, carrots, salt and pepper until tender. Remove from heat. Take out fish and flake. Cut up onion and carrots in five cups of fish stock. Add gelatine to hot stock and stir until dissolved. Add 1 teaspoon of sugar. Add the flaked fish, allow to cool, add the chopped celery or cucumber, olives and pepper. Rinse mould in cold water, fill with mixture. Chill in refrigerator. When set, insert knife round edges and turn out on platter.

Steamed Flying Fish

Steamed Flying Fish

6 boned flying fish
2 limes
2 sliced onions
pepper and salt to taste
2 tablespoons seasoning mixture
(p21)
1 teaspoon mustard
1 teaspoon vinegar
1 tablespoon flour
2 tablespoons butter
1 sliced tomato
1 cup water

Marinate the fish in a little salt and lime juice for 15-20 minutes. Drain and season the fish carefully with seasoning paste. Roll inwards from the tail end and arrange the rolled fish in a stewpan with mustard, vinegar, flour, butter, tomato, sliced onions and water. Add salt and pepper to taste and simmer gently until fish is cooked. Serve with lime slices and parsley.

Fried Flying Fish

6 boned flying fish
oil for frying
2 limes
2 tablespoons seasoning mixture
(p21)
seasoned flour (p19)
1-2 beaten eggs (optional)
1 teaspoon salt

Marinate in lime and salt for about 15 minutes. Drain well and rub with seasoning mixture in the grooves left after boning the fish. Dip in flour, then brush with egg (if used), then flour again and fry in hot shallow fat, first on the top side and then on the back of the fish fillets until brown.

Coating Batter for Frying

100g (4oz) flour
1 egg (optional) or
1/4 teaspoon salt
1/2 teaspoon baking powder
1/2 cup milk

Sift together flour and salt. Make a hole in centre of flour and add the egg and some of the milk. Mix well to a stiff consistency, adding the rest of the milk. Allow it to stand for 30 minutes. Then fry in hot fat as a blue haze rises from it. This batter is also used for Pancakes and Yorkshire Pudding.

Kedgeree

450g (1lb) cooked fish
2 tablespoons butter
1/3 cup milk
salt and pepper to taste
1 tablespoon minced onion
3 hard boiled eggs
2 cups cooked rice

Flake the fish. Chop the egg whites and add them to the melted butter, rice, fish, salt and pepper, and onion. Add milk and stir over low heat until very hot. Serve garnished with sieved egg-yolk and parsley.

Curried Shrimps

Frizzled Salt Fish

225g (1/2lb) salt fish
2 rashers bacon or slices of ham
piece red hot pepper
1-2 eggs
white pepper
75g (3oz) chopped cabbage
few blades of chives (eschalot)
1 chopped onion
sprig sweet marjoram
1 large tomato or
2 tablespoons tomato ketchup
2 tablespoons butter
fat for frying
1 tablespoon parsley (chopped)

Soak salt fish, squeeze dry and pound fine in a mortar. If fish is hard, boil first. Cut up bacon or ham, also cabbage, seasonings and mix with fish. Melt the fat in frying pan, stir in fish and seasonings. Just before removing from heat, stir in one or two beaten eggs, and remove as egg is cooked. Garnish with parsley and serve with split peas and rice.

Curried Shrimps

2 cups fresh shrimps
1 teaspoon salt
1/2 teaspoon pepper
1 cup coconut milk
fat for frying
2 tablespoons curry powder
2 tablespoons butter
1 large tomato
1 onion (chopped)
2-3 blades chives (eschalot)

Scald shrimps in boiling salted water for 2-5 minutes depending on size of shrimps. Cool and peel off heads and shells. Cut open backs and remove black vein. Wash in lime juice and salt water. Lightly brown onion in fat, add curry and cook 5 minutes. Add 1 cup of coconut milk and simmer gently for 15 minutes. Add butter, and slivers of eschalot and shrimp and simmer for 3-5 minutes. Serve hot with boiled rice.

Crab Backs

12 cooked crabs
2 teaspoons vinegar
4 tablespoons browned crumbs
1 teaspoon minced fresh hot pepper
salt
1 tablespoon minced onion
2 tablespoons butter
1/2 teaspoon curry powder

Shell crabs and mince the meat. Mix the breadcrumbs, black pepper, salt, butter, vinegar, minced pepper, onion and curry powder all with the crab meat. Fill the backs, topping with breadcrumbs and dots of butter. Bake for 15 to 20 minutes till brown.

Salt Fish Cakes

Fresh Fish vs Iced Fish

Long ago, when refrigeration was not so common in homes, the management of the Ice House in Broad Street started to freeze the local fish. They owned fishing boats and employed fishermen to get the fish for storage. My father did not like the fish and my mother always had to get freshly caught fish for his meals. One evening my mother had prepared the iced fish for the rest of the family and fried a few veal cutlets for him and placed them in a separate round dish from which she served him. He must have noticed the fried 'iced fish' as it was called and immediately started to chide her for offering him the fish which he did not like. When he realized his mistake he quickly apologized, but we the children thought he was being favoured as we had no choice but to eat the fish which our mother had prepared for us.

Salt Fish Cakes

225g (1/2lb) fish
100g (1/4lb) pumpkin or potato
100g (1/4lb) flour
2 eggs
milk to mix
1 tablespoon butter
fat for frying
breadcrumbs and flour
salt and pepper
1 tablespoon chopped onion and herbs

Soak and mince fish finely. Add pumpkin or potato, grated raw. Beat eggs. Add milk, butter, seasonings, and salt and pepper to taste and mix together. Add to the fish and mix well with the flour and make into cakes or balls. Dip in breadcrumbs and flour and fry in fat till golden brown.

Salt Fish and Melongenes (Aubergines)

225g (1/2lb) salt fish
2 blades chives
450g (1lb) melongenes
2 tablespoons butter or margarine
2 tablespoons onion (sliced)
grated cheese or breadcrumbs

Scald and clean fish. Peel, slice and boil melongenes, drain and crush. Mix with fish. Sauté seasonings, mix in butter and add to mixture. Top with butter, grated cheese or breadcrumbs. Grill or bake until brown before serving.

Sea Eggs

Those of us who knew Sea Eggs at their best a few generations ago are saddened that the delicacy is now so scarce in this generation. In my younger years sea eggs were known to be available for several months of the year. Some people used to say they could be bought in the months ending with 'rs', that is from September through December. There was no over harvesting or early taking of the young shell which has caused the terrible shortage and the outlook for the future seems to be dismal.

Long ago sea eggs were reaped at maturity, the shells were broken, the mature roes were used to fill empty shells on the beaches. Grape leaves were used like cones to cover the sea eggs. The eggs were then smoked on a wire over a fire between two rocks. After smoking they were sold to the public. The sea egg was firm and dry. Householders could then float them in salt water to remove sand, prickles and seaweed and other foreign matter and finally cook them with herbs and onions. Nowadays too much of the young sea egg is washed away in the sea during the first filling of shells resulting in much loss from the destruction of the young eggs. This delicacy seems to be lost to many generations.

Flying Fish

When flying fish was very plentiful, fishermen, after selling fish at the various fish markets, used to sell the excess fish after 6pm to householders in the nearby streets, as there was no means of refrigeration. The fishermen sold the rest of their catch from carts with lighted torches. They would go through the neighbourhood crying, "F-e-e-s-h, F-e-e-s-h". When they heard the cry, householders would come out with containers to purchase the fish. At this time of the day they were sold "all a penny" that means that you would get them to fill a bowl of your choice for 10 cents.

The point was to get rid of the fish. The household members were kept busy for several hours boning and frying the fish for the next day. People were very grateful to the fishermen for this cheap source of flying fish. In the sea egg season, the sea eggs were picked, piled in empty shells, smoked on the beach, covered with grape leaves and sold from 3 to 5 cents a shell.

In those times wages were ridiculously low and despite the apparently low price of food, many people could barely exist. There was a serious depression which culminated in the 1937 riots, after which Labour leaders like Duncan O'Neal, Grantley Adams, Hugh Springer and later Frank Walcott and others, had to work hard to introduce Labour laws and improve working conditions for the majority of the people.

Prices of some everyday foods in the 1930s

Rice, sugar, flour	4-5 cents lb
Cooking butter	60 cents lb tin
Sweet potatoes	5-6 cents lb for a 'bit'
Cheese	72 cents lb
yams, eddoes	10 cents
Plantains	4-5 cents for a bit
Flying fish	3-10 cents for a bit
Eggs	3-5 cents for a bit
Pork, any cut	20 cents lb
Small bananas	3 or 4 for a penny
Beef, any cut	24 cents lb
Mangoes	1-2 cents each
Lettuce	3-6 cents head
Golden apples	1-2 cents each
Cabbage	30-60 cents lb
Oranges	2 cents each
Tomatoes	20 cents lb
Condensed milk	6-10 cents tin
Cucumbers	2-6 cents each
Cow's milk	6 cents Dint
Onions	8-10 cents lb
Eclipse biscuits	6 for 1 cent
Small cracker	10 for 1 cent

Meat available in the Caribbean includes beef, pork, veal, lamb, mutton, offal and poultry. Wild meat or game such as agouti, lappe and wild duck and rabbit are available in some areas. Chickens, turkeys, ducks and geese are the main poultry meats used in local cookery. Meat and poultry are high quality protein foods and are also the most expensive. However, economical cuts like stewing beef, breast of lamb, and pork shoulder provide the same food value as the more expensive cuts. Variety meats (offal) such as the liver, heart and kidney etc., are especially good value for money and should be used at least once a week.

Minced meat is economical and useful for making pies, rissoles and hamburgers. Dried peas and beans may be mixed with it in dishes and thus improve their nutritional value.

Pork is very popular in meat cookery in the area, even the head and feet (trotters) are used for making souse. Mutton and goat meat are used in curries, also chicken, especially by sections of the population who, for religious and other reasons, do not eat pork and beef.

Fresh meat should have a good colour without an unpleasant odour. Pork flesh should be pale with firm fat. It should always be thoroughly cooked. Beef should be deep red streaked with fat, but veal should be pale and leaner with less fat. Lamb and mutton should be paler than beef with solid white fat.

Avoid par-cooking meat for later use. It may become a source of food poisoning. Cook it thoroughly, cover and keep it in a refrigerator, and reheat before using. Unwrap frozen meat before storing in a refrigerator. After the meat has thawed out it should never be re-frozen.

Methods of cooking meat

Oven roasting, grilling, frying, stewing and braising are the popular ways of cooking meat. In whichever way it is prepared, the temperature should be low to moderate heat. Better cuts are roasted, grilled or fried; cheaper and tougher cuts are stewed and braised, thus being allowed to simmer until tender.

Large cuts of fresh meat to be served cold are put in hot water with seasonings, simmered and sliced when cool. Salt meat is soaked beforehand and cooked in cold water.

When doing pressure or rotisserie cooking, follow the instructions given with the equipment.

Whenever a meat thermometer is used in roasting meat, be sure that it is pushed into the meat so that the tip of it reaches the centre of the thickest muscle and not in the fat.

Roasting: Season meat, place in oven at 170°C, 325°F or Gas 3 with fat side up. Leave meat uncovered. It is unnecessary to baste it or to put water in the pan. The meat will brown as it cooks. Roasting time for beef is 25-40 minutes per 450g (1lb) depending on how well done it is required. Pork needs to be well done, about 45 minutes to 450g (1lb). Veal requires 30 minutes and lamb 35-40 minutes to 450g (1lb).

Broiling (grilling): Follow directions for your cooker. Turn meat once only. Time varies according to the thickness of the steaks being cooked.

Frying: A heavy frying pan is useful for thin beef steaks, veal cutlets, pork chops and liver which are usually fried in a small amount of fat.

Stewing: Tougher joints are cut in serving pieces, seasoned, browned in hot fat, covered with water and allowed to simmer. Vegetables are added towards the end of the cooking period.

Braising and Pot Roasting: Pieces of meat are seasoned with salt and pepper and browned on all sides in hot fat. Water is added in small amounts as required. Keep the saucepan covered and cook very slowly until tender.

Beef Stew and Vegetables

Beef Stew and Vegetables

450g (1lb) stewing steak
15g (1/2oz) flour
pepper and salt to taste
1 large onion
100g (1/4lb) carrots or turnips
2 cups water
25g (1oz) fat for frying
few garden tomatoes

Cut meat into serving pieces. Slice onion. When fat is smoking hot, fry meat on both sides till brown. Lift out and keep hot. Fry the onion, stir in flour, and fry slowly to a rich brown. Add the water, boil up, add salt and skim. Return meat to pan. Add diced vegetables to the stew and allow to simmer for 2 hours. Lift meat on to a hot dish, arrange vegetables at each end, and pour the sauce over.

Beef Loaf

450g (1lb) minced meat
2 tablespoons chopped sweet pepper
3/4 cup breadcrumbs
1 beaten egg
1 small can tomato soup
1 1/2 teaspoons salt
1/2 cup finely chopped onion
1 teaspoon chopped mixed herbs

Combine all ingredients and mix well. Shape mixture into a loaf in shallow baking dish. Garnish with sweet pepper slices after baking in a moderate oven for about 1 hour.

Barbequed Steak

Choose porterhouse, T-bone, tenderloin or sirloin steak, cut 2.5 cm (1in) thick. Trim off the fat to avoid it burning and dripping onto the flames. Marinate the meat in a BBQ seasoning and/or BBQ sauce with freshly ground black pepper to taste. Place steaks on preheated grill rack, near the heat for thin steaks - farther from heat for thicker ones. Brown the top side, sprinkle lightly with salt and pepper, then the other side; season, and serve very hot. For 2.5cm (1in) steaks, allow 5-8 minutes each side for rare, and 6-10 minutes for medium. For 3.5cm (1 1/2in) steaks, allow 8-10 minutes each side for rare, 10-15 minutes for medium, and longer in each case for well done, when meat should look grey.

Stuffed Pork Shoulder

Baked Pork

2.7-3.5kg (6-8lb) pork loin
1 teaspoon white pepper
2 teaspoons salt
2 teaspoons sugar
seasoning mixture (p21)
25g (1oz) butter

Wash the meat and dry thoroughly. With a sharp knife, make deep gashes in the meat in several places. Rub the joint thoroughly with the salt and white pepper. Cover and put it aside for 15-20 minutes. Rub some seasoning mixture into the gashes made in the meat. Baste the joint with the butter and put into a roasting pan, uncovered, in a moderate oven allowing it to bake 25 minutes for each pound and 25 minutes extra, turning and basting occasionally with the dripping from the pan. During the last half hour of baking, sprinkle the skin side with the sugar, and raise the oven temperature to 200°C, 400°F or Gas 6 to allow the skin to become crisp and brown. Serve the roast with Mock Apple Sauce and Brown Gravy.

Mock Apple Sauce

450g (1lb) green pawpaw
1/4 cup hot water
50g (2oz) sugar
1 tablespoon lime juice

Peel and cut the pawpaw in pieces. Place in a saucepan with water to cover and bring it to the boil. Throw off this water, drain and add 1/4 cup of water and the sugar, allowing the pawpaw to simmer until it is very soft. Remove it from the heat; add one tablespoon of lime juice and beat it with a wooden spoon until smooth. Serve one to two tablespoons with each serving of baked pork.

Brown Gravy

2 onions
pepper and salt to taste
2 tablespoons dripping
sediment from baked pork
few slices tomato or
1 teaspoon tomato paste
1 cup hot water or stock

Wash and slice the onions and place them into the hot sediment dripping into the pan, sprinkling over the flour to brown well. Skim off any fat and add one cup of hot water and the tomatoes. Stir well and simmer until it thickens. Add salt and pepper to taste.

Stuffed Pork Shoulder

Bone a shoulder or hand of pork. Rub over with salt and pepper. Fill with stuffing. Tie up firmly and bake slowly in moderate oven until brown, turning over and basting with some of its dripping. Raise the heat for the last 15-20 minutes to brown the skin, and allow to become crisp. Serve with gravy.

Stuffing
1 cup bread or biscuit crumbs
1 tablespoon raisins or sweet pickles
2 tablespoons fat for frying
black pepper and salt to taste
1 chopped onion
1 beaten egg
2 rashers of bacon cut in pieces
2 teaspoons dried sage or mixed herbs
1 clove garlic (chopped)
milk or water to moisten

Mix all ingredients and fry lightly in 2 tablespoons of fat. Cool a little and stuff joint carefully.

48

Baked Ham

Curing Ham

Several years ago in the 1980s, I had an old refrigerator changed into a ham curer. Someone helped me to remove some of the shelves. Two hooks for hanging the ham and a vent for the smoke to exit were placed at the top and a coal pot placed in the bottom flat. In it I put hickory chips to smoke which one could buy in the supermarket. The pork leg had to first be prepared with special brine and rubbed with salt cure both of which were sold in the supermarket at that time. The result was very successful and the hams very flavourful. I made several until I could no longer get the materials for curing preparation.

Picnic Shoulder of Ham

one 2.25kg (5lb) picnic ham shoulder
3/4 cup vinegar
few whole cloves
thin garlic slices

Cut slits here and there in the meat about 1cm (1/2in) deep and insert the slices of garlic. Place it in a saucepan and cover with cold water. Add the vinegar and whole cloves. Cover and simmer for about 3 hours. Skin the meat, remove from liquid and bake at 180°C, 350°F or Gas 4 for about 15-20 minutes. Use the following glaze:

Mustard glaze
Mix together 1 cup brown sugar, 1 teaspoon dry mustard, 2 or 3 tablespoons ham fat or dripping. Baste this on the meat before baking.

Baked Ham

Place the ham, fat side up, on a rack in a shallow oven pan. Bake, in a slow oven for 2-3 1/2 hours allowing 15-20 minutes per 450g (1lb). Half an hour before it is finished, remove the ham from the oven, skin it, pour off the dripping, score the ham fat in diamond shapes. Stick in whole cloves and pour over it some mustard glaze (as used for Picnic Shoulder). Canned cooked hams may be baked and glazed as for Baked Ham allowing about 20-35 minutes in the oven at 180°C, 350°F or Gas 4.

50

Mixed Grill

Baked Chicken

1.3-1.8kg (3-4lb) chicken
2 cups coarse breadcrumbs
1 medium onion
giblets (liver, gizzard, heart)
1 sprig thyme or marjoram
1 bacon rasher
hot pepper and salt to taste
fat from chicken or oil
few raisins or capers
few garden tomatoes (small)
1 teaspoon soy sauce (optional)
1 tablespoon butter

Moisten the crumbs with water to soften, but do not make into a paste. Fry the chicken fat with the giblets and bacon cut in pieces. Cook for about 5 minutes. Add the chopped onion, tomatoes and other seasonings. Stir in the damp crumbs mixing in well; add butter and cook for about 5 minutes more. Cool the mixture and stuff the chicken, sewing or skewering to close the opening. Brush with butter or bacon fat. Place in roasting pan, breast upwards. Allow 1/2 hour per 450g (1lb) at 200°C, 400°F or Gas 6.

Mixed Grill

2 lamb kidneys
4 bacon rashers
4 lamb chops
4 tomatoes
100g (4oz) mushrooms
salt and pepper
1/2 teaspoon celery salt
1/2 teaspoon garlic salt

Rub lamb chops and kidneys with basic marinade mixture. Drain and brown lamb chops on one side under hot grill. Lightly fry kidneys and mushrooms with bacon rashers. Brown other side of chops. Arrange kidneys, mushrooms and halved tomatoes around them. Sprinkle with salt and pepper. Arrange bacon rashers on top and cook under medium heat until chops are finished.

Grilled Pork Chops

6 pork chops
white pepper
garlic salt

Season chops well, rubbing over with garlic salt and pepper or season with some basic marinade. Put under grill with medium flame allowing about 25 minutes for cooking; turn up the flame during the last 5-6 minutes for browning. Put them in a covered dish in a moderate oven to cook through for about 20 minutes. Serve with caramel sweet potatoes (p67).

Chicken Salad

Curried Mutton, Lamb or Goat

900g (2lb) mutton
225g (1/2lb) carrots
3 onions
2 tablespoons curry powder
1 bunch herbs
1 teaspoon sugar
1 clove garlic
2 tablespoons tomato ketchup
1 dessertspoon salt or to taste
1 tablespoon fat
water to cover

Cut meat in pieces, fry lightly in fat, add curry powder and simmer in water (enough to cover the meat) with seasonings until meat is nearly tender (about 1 1/2 hours). Dice carrots and add. Continue cooking until meat and carrots are tender.

Stewed Chicken

1.35kg (3lb) chicken
salt and pepper to taste
1 clove garlic
1 tablespoon vinegar
1 teaspoon sugar
2 tablespoons tomato sauce
2 medium sliced onions
3 tablespoons fat
2 teaspoons soy sauce
1/2 cup diced carrots
about 2 cups water
few whole cloves

Cut the chicken limbs and breast into 12 pieces, and the bony residue of carcass in 4. Marinate these in vinegar and salt for about 15 minutes. Fry the crushed garlic and sugar in the oil until very brown, then remove garlic. Brown the chicken pieces in the hot fat. Drain off excess fat, add water and other ingredients and allow to simmer for about 1 hour.

Chicken Salad

4 cups cooked diced chicken
1/2 cup French dressing
1 cup chopped celery
1/2 cup mayonnaise or salad dressing
1 cup chopped sweet pepper
1/2 cup chicken stock
2 tablespoons grated onion
salt and pepper to taste
lettuce leaves, parsley, etc.

Mix together dressings, stock and seasonings and pour over the chicken mixture, blending thoroughly. Chill in refrigerator until required; then serve on a bed of lettuce. Garnish with parsley or as desired.

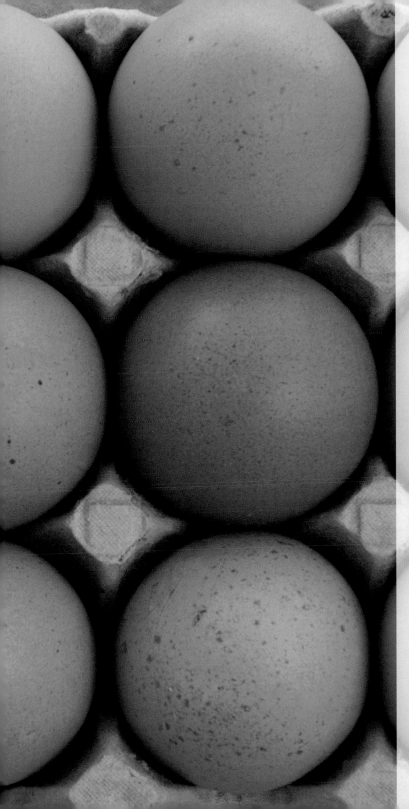

Milk, Egg & Cheese Cookery

Milk is the most important food for infants, children and adults in sickness or health. It is very easily digested. It contains 88% water and has more nutrients than any other food. It is rich in bone and body-building material but is deficient in iron and Vitamins C and D. Vitamin D, however, is synthesized in the body from the sunshine, so there is no serious lack of this vitamin in the Caribbean.

In some Caribbean islands there is a general shortage of fresh cows' milk, although dairy farms are on the increase, but some pasteurized milk is available. UHT long life milk is now available everywhere .

Condensed milk is widely used but should not be substituted for fresh milk. Because of the large amount of sugar it contains, it has the advantage of keeping for several days without refrigeration.

Evaporated milk is pure sterilized tinned milk which has half the water removed and may be reconstituted by mixing one part evaporated milk to one part water.

Whole milk powder is pure dried milk with the water removed to allow for long storage in tins. Follow the directions on the tin for reconstituting it.

Dried skimmed milk powder is dried like whole milk powder, but has most of the fat removed in processing. It is rich in calcium and protein. It is inexpensive, good value for money, and should be more widely used, especially in milk cookery.

The value of milk in any form cannot be over-estimated. It may be used as a beverage, plain or flavoured, with porridge or cereal, in custards, soups, ice cream and with stewed fruit.

Sour milk should not be thrown away. It may be used in cakes and scones with a little bicarbonate of soda as a raising agent.

Cheese

Cheese is a milk product rich in protein and fat. Cheddar cheese is the most economical to buy in the Caribbean. Cream cheese is rich in fat and more expensive. All kinds of cheese should be kept cool and placed in the refrigerator. Mould on cheese may be pared off and discarded; the cheese is still wholesome. Hard pieces of cheese may be grated and used in cheese cookery. Always cook cheese dishes at low or medium temperatures. Quick cooking at high temperatures makes it tough and stringy. Cheese is useful for combining with main dishes, soups, salads sandwiches etc., and adds extra nourishment.

Butter

Butter is also made from cows' milk and is about 4/5ths fat. It is salted during its manufacture. In the Caribbean area ordinary butter is often referred to as table butter to distinguish it from cooking butter which is a highly salted orange-coloured pure butter imported from the UK. It is widely used in meat and fish cookery and sometimes in cake and bread making. Imported margarine which is cheaper, is obtained in similar form. This butter and margarine have a cheesy taste which adds much to the appetizing flavour of dishes in which they are used. The salt preserves it for a long period and refrigeration is not so necessary.

Eggs

Eggs may be considered with dairy produce and cheese as they are so often used together in foods. These are rich in high quality protein; the yolk also contains some Vitamin A, iron and fat.

Like milk and cheese, they must be kept cool. If refrigerated, cool them to room temperature before beating them for making cakes. Test them in a bowl of water for freshness. A stale egg floats to the top, a fresh one will sink to the bottom. Eggs will retain their freshness for 2-3 weeks without refrigeration if kept in a box of sand and turned daily.

Eggs are graded and sold in a variety of sizes. Discretion must be used in buying them in different places. Farm eggs are guaranteed fresher than those sold in grocery shops. To ensure freshness, break each separately in a saucer before mixing with other ingredients.

Low or medium heat is used when cooking eggs. Popular methods of cooking are boiled (soft or hard), scrambled, fried, poached, or omelettes.

Cream or White Sauces

1. Thin sauce for soups and vegetables (1 cup)

1 tablespoon butter or margarine
1/4 teaspoon salt
2 tablespoons flour
1 cup milk

2. Medium sauce for scalloped dishes and fish pie or as a sauce (1 cup)

2 tablespoons butter or margarine
1/4 teaspoon salt
1 tablespoon flour
1 cup milk

3. Thick sauce for soufflés and croquettes (1 cup)

3 tablespoons butter or margarine
1/4 teaspoon salt
4 tablespoons flour
1 cup milk

To cook the sauces, melt butter or margarine in saucepan over low heat. Blend in flour and salt. Add milk all at once. Cook, stirring constantly with a wooden spoon until the mixture thickens.
Cook for 2 minutes.

Parsley Sauce

For Parsley Sauce, add 1 tablespoon chopped parsley to 1 cup Medium Sauce. Serve with fish or vegetables.

Mustard Sauce

For Mustard Sauce, add 1 1/2 tablespoons prepared mustard to 1 cup Medium Sauce. Serve with fish.

Cheese Sauce

For Cheese Sauce add 1 cup grated Cheddar cheese to 1 cup Medium Sauce. Stir until cheese is melted. Serve with omelette or vegetables.

Cheese Strata

8 slices bread or toast
4 eggs (slightly beaten)
1/4 cup butter or margarine
2 1/2 cups milk
2 1/2 cups grated cheese
1 teaspoon salt
1/4 teaspoon mustard

Trim crusts from bread, butter each slice and divide in 4. Place alternate layers of bread and cheese in buttered baking dish and finish with layer of cheese. Mix eggs, milk and seasonings and pour over layers. Bake in a slow oven for 45 minutes. Cool a little and cut in squares for serving.

Cream Soups

Cream of Spinach Soup

450g (1 lb) young spinach leaves
1 onion (chopped)
4 cups water
salt and pepper to taste
1 tablespoon tomato ketchup
2 cups cream sauce

Wash leaves well and boil with water, salt, pepper and onion until tender. Strain and rub through a sieve. Stir in tomato ketchup. Add 2 cups of cream sauce, heat slowly without boiling and serve.

Cream of Potato Soup

2 cups diced cooked potatoes
1 tablespoon chopped sweet pepper
2 cups cream sauce (1)
1 teaspoon salt
1 cup milk and water

Mix all ingredients in a saucepan. Stir well, heat and serve with pieces of chives or parsley.

Macaroni Cheese

Baked Custard

3-4 eggs
3 tablespoons sugar
2-2 1/2 cups milk
pinch of salt
1/2 teaspoon grated nutmeg or
vanilla essence
1 teaspoon butter

Beat eggs lightly with the other ingredients. Put into a greased baking dish. Sprinkle a little nutmeg on the top, if used. Dot butter on. Place dish in a pan of hot water in the oven. Cook at low heat, about 140°C/275°F or Gas 1 for about one hour or until finished and set firmly. This custard may also be steamed in the top of a double boiler until set.

Macaroni Cheese

225g (1/2lb) macaroni (cooked)
1 medium tomato (sliced)
200g (8oz) cheese, grated
1 small onion (sliced or chopped)
2 tablespoons butter
1 cup milk
2 eggs
salt and pepper to taste

Butter a baking dish and put alternate layers of macaroni, grated cheese, sliced onion and tomato, finishing with a layer of macaroni. Pour the milk, beaten eggs, salt and pepper mixture over the food, add a little grated cheese and dot with butter. Bake in a moderate oven for about 1/2 hour.

Cheese Soufflé

1 cup soufflé sauce (p59)
1/2 cup biscuit or bread crumbs
1/2 cup grated cheese
3 eggs (separated)
1/4 teaspoonful white pepper
1 small minced onion

Mix all ingredients together except the eggs. Beat the yolks and add them to the mixture. Then carefully fold in egg whites, previously beaten, until stiff. Pour in a baking dish and bake in moderate oven for about 1 hour. Serve immediately.

Bacon and Fried Eggs

Scrambled Eggs

Use 1-2 eggs per person.

6 eggs
1/4 teaspoon white pepper
1/3 cup milk
2 tablespoons butter or margarine
3/4 teaspoon salt

Beat eggs lightly with a fork. Add salt, pepper and milk. Mix well. Heat butter in pan over low heat. Pour in mixture and as it begins to set, use a spatula to turn mixture until it sets throughout, but remove it from the heat while still moist and serve at once. Chopped onion, grated cheese, shredded fried fish or tomato may be added for variation.

Bacon and Fried Eggs

6 eggs
6 (or more) rashers bacon
salt, pepper
Worstershire sauce (optional)

Remove bacon rinds if necessary. Place rashers in a warm pan and fry slowly without using extra fat. Fry until the fat is cooked or seems transparent, lightly brown on both sides, but not crisp. Remove bacon from the pan and put aside to keep warm. Fry eggs in the bacon fat removing any fried bits adhering to the pan. Add extra oil if necessary. Fry eggs one at a time, carefully breaking them in a saucer and slipping them into the pan. Sprinkle with salt and pepper. As soon as white sets, ease round the edges with the spatula and spoon the fat over the egg until a white film forms over the yolk. Remove it from the pan and fry the other eggs. Lay a rasher of bacon on each egg and serve hot.

Creole Omelette

1 onion (minced)
green pepper
1 tablespoon tomato (minced) or
1 teaspoon ketchup
4 beaten eggs
100g (1/4lb) ham
oil for frying
1/4 cup breadcrumbs (soaked in milk)
1 clove garlic
1 tablespoon butter

Sauté minced onion, tomato and chopped garlic. Add breadcrumbs, remove from heat and allow to cool. Add beaten eggs. Mix well and add bits of ham and green pepper. Put butter in pan. When hot pour in omelette and fry over low flame. Turn the whole omelette over once, fold in half or fold in the four sides to leave a small window in the centre. Serve hot.

Vegetable Omelette

Any number of vegetables may be added to an omlette:
brocolli or cauliflower
mushrooms
asparagus
spinach or pak choy
okras
This provides an excellent healthy start to the day.

Energy Foods

There is a great variety of these foods from which to choose. Root crops, cereal foods, other starchy fruits, fresh and dried peas and beans (pulses) all contribute to our wealth of energy foods. They are a valuable source of calories as they contain a high percentage of starch converted to sugar by the body. Quantities eaten should be limited since too much sugar causes obesity and diabetes. Yams, sweet potatoes, tannia, eddoes, dasheen, and cassava are among the commonly used root crops. Plantains, green bananas and breadfruit are other favourites. Dried peas and beans not only supply calories but supplement the animal proteins which are scarce and expensive. Imported English potatoes are still used widely and assist with the diet especially when root crops are in short supply.

Rice, a cereal food, is however the basic starchy food eaten throughout the Caribbean area. It is cheap and always available as it is grown in the area, chiefly in Guyana. Rice is also rich in calcium and has good supplies of iron and protein and B vitamins. Brown or unpolished rice is superior nutritionally, but white rice is in greater demand and is now fortified in some countries. Pulses are used regularly in rice dishes and, with small amounts of meat or fish added, they provide excellent dishes.

Green corn or maize is boiled and served on the cob as a vegetable, and dried corn is ground into meal and cooked in porridge and other dishes. The yellow corn contains carotene and is better than the white variety. The protein in corn is not a useful food supplement. Macaroni products or pasta are used in dishes to add variety to meals.

All starchy vegetables may be boiled in salted water and served in slices or mashed and buttered. Cook them in a covered saucepan to save vitamin loss and, whenever possible, cook them in the skins, e.g. sweet potatoes.

Baked Stuffed Breadfruit

Energy Foods

Scalloped Sweet Potato and Onions

900g (2lb) medium sized potatoes
1/2 teaspoon salt
100g (1/4lb) onions
1/2 teaspoon white pepper
3/4 cup milk
1 tablespoon grated cheese
50g (2oz) flour
25g (1oz) butter

Parboil sweet potatoes, peel and slice thinly. Also slice onions. Grease a baking dish with butter. Put the potatoes and onions in it in alternate layers. Sprinkle between layers with a mixture of flour, salt and white pepper. Dot with butter and grated cheese and almost cover the vegetables with milk. Bake in moderate oven. Yams and English potatoes may be cooked in the same way.

Caramel Sweet Potato

4 cups cooked and mashed sweet potatoes
marshmallows
1/2 cup orange or pineapple juice
3 tablespoons butter
1 teaspoon peanut butter
1/4 cup sugar (brown)

Dissolve sugar in butter over low heat. Add this along with the juice and peanut butter to mashed potatoes. Put into a greased baking dish and arrange marshmallows on top of mixture. Bake in a moderate oven until marshmallows are spread and light brown.

Baked Stuffed Breadfruit

1 breadfruit (not over-ripe)
1 tomato
225g (1/2lb) fresh meat
salt and pepper to taste
100g (1/4lb) salt meat
2 tablespoons butter
1 onion
2-3 blades chive (eschalot)

Peel breadfruit and parboil whole in salted water. Lightly fry meat in some fat and seasonings. Cut up meat and mince. Cut off stem of breadfruit, peel and core it well. Fill it with meat mixture mixed with butter. Bake in a greased dish in a moderate oven for about 45 minutes. Baste fruit with butter and serve hot.

Pigeon Peas

Pigeon Peas and Rice

2 cups rice
4 cups water
salt to taste
bunch of herbs
1 tablespoon butter
100g (1/4lb) salt meat (optional) cut
in pieces
2 cups pigeon peas
1 tablespoon lime juice
1 hot pepper
1 large tomato

Boil peas with seasonings and salt
meat, if used, for 20 minutes. Then
sprinkle in rice, lime juice and
crushed tomato. Add butter and
cover saucepan and boil over a
moderate heat at first, then allow to
steam over low heat until all the
water is absorbed and grains are
soft (about 1/2 hour). Serve hot.
Any fresh green peas or beans may
be substituted. Remove whole
pepper before serving.

Curried Green Bananas

8 green bananas (medium)
1 teaspoon hot pepper sauce
1 cup coconut milk
salt and pepper to taste
2 tablespoons curry powder
1 beaten egg
25g (1oz) margarine or butter
boiled rice

Fry curry in margarine for 2
minutes. Peel and slice bananas,
place in margarine and curry and
brown lightly. Add pepper, salt and
coconut milk and simmer gently for
1/2 hour. Stir in beaten egg. Serve
with boiled rice.

Pickled Breadfruit

1 breadfruit
salt
lime juice
chopped onion
parsley

Peel, core and cut an under-ripe
breadfruit in 1cm (1/2in) slices. Boil
in salt water. Prepare pickle of lime
juice, chopped onion, salt and
pepper to taste. Pour this over
breadfruit slices in a dish. Keep
warm and when ready to serve,
spread with butter. Salt fish or meat
is a good accompaniment for this
dish. Green bananas may also be
pickled.

70

These embrace the green and yellow vegetables which are of special importance because they provide carotene (pro Vitamin A) and Vitamin C and some calcium. Carrots, pumpkins, red sweet peppers, avocados, okras, also the dark green leaves of spinach, cabbage, lettuce, kale, sweet potato, beet and turnip, watercress and parsley are all good sources of carotene. Vitamin C is present in all green vegetables but is very quickly lost from the vegetable after it is picked or cut from the garden. Storing, especially in warm climates, causes further reduction or loss of Vitamin C.

All fresh fruits, especially the yellow varieties such as mango, banana, pawpaw, pineapple, citrus varieties, avocado pear, plums, garden cherries, golden apple, monkey apple, cashew, guavas, etc., are rich in carotene, iron and Vitamin C in varying proportions. They are usually eaten raw, but are also used in drinks, cooked in jams and jellies and used in many ways in desserts. Raw fruit should always be carefully washed before use. Storing of fruits, like vegetables, reduces the flavour and vitamin content.

It is very necessary, therefore, to obtain vegetables and fruits which are garden fresh and young. If they must be stored for a few days, keep them in plastic bags in a refrigerator or cool place.

Cooking and preparing vegetables

Rinse all vegetables quickly in cold water. Cook them in the minimum of fast boiling salted water. Any residue of water after cooking should be used for gravies to save the soluble Vitamin C content. Plan the meal preparation so that green vegetables are cooked just before the meal is to be served, as exposure to air and heating over a long period cause further deterioration. Cooking of vegetables in a steamer or pressure cooker helps to preserve their nutritive qualities. The use of bicarbonate of soda in cooking water must also be strictly avoided.

Take great care in the preparation of leafy green vegetables for raw salads. They should be rinsed leaf by leaf to remove any sand particles, or grubs, but no vegetables should be left soaking in water. Drain the salad greens in a colander or salad shaker, and dry carefully on a clean towel. All greens for salad must be young and in perfect condition. A salad cream or French dressing may be used for seasoning just before serving. Vegetables may be cut or shredded, but avoid grating them as they lose crispness as well as vitamins. Use lettuce leaves whole or tear them apart. After preparing salads, cover them until they are to be served. Green vegetables are also important in the diet for their cellulose content which is not digestible, but acts as roughage, stimulates the digestive tract and therefore has a laxative effect.

Dehydrated, frozen and canned vegetables and fruits

Frozen vegetables are very carefully selected from sound produce. They are cooked very quickly by a special method, and quickly frozen to retain the vitamin content. They are therefore specially favoured for their superior quality to the average market vegetables. There is little labour in their preparation and they are an excellent substitute for home grown vegetables. Be sure to cook them quickly before they are thawed out.

Canned vegetables and fruit are also as valuable as those freshly cooked. During the process of canning, some of the vitamin content is drawn into the liquid in the can, so it should also be used when cooking. After cans are opened, use the contents as quickly as possible.

Stuffed Sweet Peppers

Bok Choy Salad

1/2 kilo (1 head) Bok Choy (Chinese
Cabbage) (fat stalks)
2 pkgs of 3 minute noodles
1/2cup sliced almonds
3/4cup sesame seeds

1/3 cup olive or peanut oil
1/4 cup brown sugar
2 tablespoons soya sauce
1/4 cup apple cider vinegar
2 tablespoons oil
1 teaspoon garlic powder
1 cup purple grapes

Wash and chop bok choy and
refrigerate in plastic bag in fridge.
Sauté noodles in oil with almonds,
sesame seeds and garlic powder till
brown.
Boil sugar, soy sauce and apple cider
vinegar in pan with oil just until
sugar dissolves.
To serve mix bok choy, noodle mix
and sauce together in a salad bowl
and decorate with purple grapes.

Fried Cabbage/Stir Fry Vegetables

225g (1/2lb) cabbage/vegetables
1 tablespoon butter
salt and pepper to taste
1 tablespoon olive oil
3 bacon rashers (optional)

Wash and shred cabbage/vegetables
and sprinkle with a little salt and
pepper. Cut up bacon and fry in fat.
Put in cabbage/vegetables turning
it/them over during cooking until
finished. Remove from heat, stir in
butter and serve with fried rice.

Stuffed Sweet Peppers

4 sweet peppers
2 teaspoons tomato sauce
1 stalk celery or 225g (1/2lb) chocho
1 teaspoon cornflour
325g (3/4lb) cooked minced meat
breadcrumbs
2 tablespoons onion
salt and pepper

Cut the peppers in half and remove
the seeds. Chop the vegetables and
mix with the minced meat. Add the
tomato sauce, cornflour and salt to
taste, and mix well. Stuff the
peppers with this filling, and bake
them for 1/2 hour in a moderate
oven.

Cucumber & Avocado Salad

Moulded Vegetable Salad

2 tablespoons powdered gelatine
3/4 cup chopped sweet pepper
1/2 cup sugar
1/2 cup vinegar
1 teaspoon salt
2 tablespoons lime juice
1 1/2 cups boiling water
2 cups finely shredded cabbage
1 1/2 cups cold water
1 cup chopped celery or cucumber
few stuffed green olives
lettuce leaves

Mix gelatine, sugar and salt. Add boiling water and stir till gelatine dissolves. Add cold water, vinegar and lime juice; chill till partially set. Add vegetables, pour into ring mould. Chill till firm. Unmould on lettuce leaves. If desired, fill ring with tiny whole cooked carrots marinated in French or Italian dressing.
Alternatively, chill gelatine till partially set; pour 1/2 cup of gelatine into mould. Arrange trios of stuffed green olive slices in mould and chill till firm. Add vegetables to remaining gelatine and pour over. Chill till set.

Tossed Green Salad

1 large head lettuce
1 stalk celery
1 cucumber
sprig of escallion (chives, eschalot)
2 or 3 tomatoes
French dressing
1 sweet pepper

Wash the lettuce and dry on a towel. Place in salad bowl. Mix with pared and sliced cucumber, tomatoes and sweet pepper. Cut the escallion or chives and celery in rings. Toss well with French dressing.
Serve chilled.

Coleslaw

Shred 3 cups cabbage very finely, using a chef's knife or grater. Cover and chill to make crisp. Add 1/4 cup chopped green pepper or minced onion or 1 cup grated carrot and 1/2 cup raisins. Toss in salad dressing before serving.

Cucumber & Avocado Salad

1 avocado pear
1 tablespoon lime juice
1 cucumber
salt and pepper to taste
slices of sweet pepper (red)
1 teaspoon minced onion
lettuce and parsley

Peel and slice the cucumber; season with salt, pepper, lime juice, minced onion and pieces of red pepper to taste. Pile the slices in the middle of a salad dish on a bed of crisp lettuce and arrange the avocado slices around. Garnish with slices of sweet pepper and pieces of parsley.

Pineapple Fritters & Spinach Cakes

Cornmeal Fritters

1/2 cup cornmeal
1 egg
1/2 cup flour
1 cup milk
1 teaspoon baking powder
2 tablespoons margarine
1/4 teaspoon salt
few drops vanilla
3 tablespoons sugar

Sieve salt, flour and baking powder
in a bowl. Put in beaten egg and milk
by degrees, after rubbing the
margarine into the flour mixture.
Beat until smooth. Drop by
spoonfuls in frying pan and fry in
hot fat. Drain on absorbent paper
before serving.

Spinach Cakes

150g (6oz) spinach or bhagi
1 tablespoon chopped onion
1 egg
1/2 teaspoon salt
1/2 teaspoon pepper
1/2 cup breadcrumbs
2 tablespoons butter
1/2 cup flour
1/2 cup milk
1/2 teaspoon baking powder
oil for frying

Wash spinach leaves well and shred
finely with a knife. Add beaten egg,
onion and melted butter, then stir in
dry ingredients sifted together. Add
milk to make a very thick batter. Fry
in hot oil till golden brown. Drain
before serving.

Pineapple Fritters

coating batter (p35)
12 slices pineapple (fresh or tinned)
fat for frying
castor sugar

Make the batter. Drain the pineapple
well. Dip each slice into batter and
then using a skewer, lower the slice
into the deep fat which should be
just hazing. Cook until crisp and
nicely browned. Drain; dredge with
castor sugar and serve at once. If
liked, serve with pineapple sauce
made from the syrup in the tin by
simmering over a medium heat until
it reduces by half..
Allow 2 fritters for each helping.

Coconut Tarts

Popular Desserts

A variety of desserts are used to accompany the spicy and often highly seasoned Caribbean dishes. Cold desserts are most popular and provide contrast for hot meals in a warm climate. Choose a refrigerator dessert, a gelatine mixture, a frozen dessert or a chilled fruit salad. Fancy cakes and pies are often favoured and sometimes hot desserts are suitable with some menus.

Fresh Fruit

Fresh Fruit Salad

1 grapefruit
1 seedless orange
few slices of pineapple
few garden cherries
1 dessert mango (Bombay or Julie)
1 cup sugar
1 1/2 cups water
1 tablespoon sherry

Boil sugar and water together till syrup is formed. Set aside to cool. Wash and peel fruit, discard seeds, and cut all into neat pieces. Mix fruit in a glass dish. Pour the syrup over the fruit. Chill and add sherry just before serving.

Grapefruit or Orange Baskets

1 grapefruit or large orange
3-4 garden cherries
1 slice fresh pineapple
1 tablespoon lime juice
1 slice dessert mango
50g (2oz) granulated sugar
few slices of banana
1/3 cup water or fruit juice

To prepare a grapefruit or orange basket, wash the fruit and cut it from both sides almost in half leaving about 2cm (3/4in) uncut towards the centre. Cut the two top quarters downwards leaving the uncut 2cm (3/4in) now about halfway around the circumference and remove the quarters. With a fruit knife cut the fruit from the semi-circle thus forming a handle. Core and remove the fruit from the basket which is now cleaned by scraping out all the pith well. Dice the pineapple and mango; add banana slices and some of the grapefruit sections, squeezing the lime juice over and mixing together in a dish. Now pour over the mixture a light cool syrup previously made by boiling the sugar and water together until it is slightly thick. Fill the basket with the mixture and garnish it with sliced cherries. Chill before serving and if desired, tie a coloured ribbon to the handle for decoration.

Floating Island

600ml (1 pint) milk (2 cups)
sugar to taste
3 eggs (separated)
2-3 tablespoons soft guava jelly
1 teaspoon vanilla essence

Make a custard with the milk and egg yolks adding sugar to taste and essence. Refer to method on page 27. Cool and pour into a glass dish. Warm the guava jelly slightly to soften. Beat the egg whites stiffly and lightly fold in the jelly a little at a time. Drop spoons of mixture on to the custard to make rough shapes. Serve very cold.

Orange Trifle

Orange or Pineapple Trifle

1 Swiss roll or small sponge cake
(sliced thinly)
1 cup fresh orange or pineapple
pieces
wineglass of sherry or rum
1 1/2 cups custard sauce (See page 89)
fruit syrup
few fresh garden cherries
jam
peanuts (crushed)

Spread some jam on the sponge
slices and arrange them in alternate
layers with the fruit and nuts in a
glass dish. Moisten each layer with
sherry and fruit juice, adding some
custard sauce. Finish with layer of
custard. Decorate top with fresh
garden cherries and pieces of fruit.
Alternatively, a meringue may be
used on top before decorating.

Meringue
To 2 stiffly beaten egg whites, add 4
tablespoons granulated sugar
gradually with 1 teaspoon of lime
juice. Whip until mixture makes
stiff peaks and add to top of trifle.
These may be baked in a very slow
oven to make it crisp for about 1 1/2
hours.

Gelatine Desserts - Guava Whip

3/4 cup sugar
1 cup fresh guava pulp
1 tablespoon powdered gelatine
2 egg whites
3/4 cup water
1 cup coconut cream (optional)
1 tablespoon lemon or lime juice
1/4 teaspoon salt

Soak gelatine in 1/4 cup water. Add
remainder of water to sugar and
heat almost to boiling point.
Remove from heat, add gelatine, stir
till dissolved. Cool. Press guava
pulp through sieve. Add salt, lemon
juice and gradually beat in cooled
syrup. Chill and when it begins to
thicken, fold in coconut (if used)
and stiffly beaten egg whites.
Mould and chill. Decorate with
shredded coconut and fresh
deseeded cherries. Other fruit
purees may be used for whips.

Mango Cream Mould

1 cup mango pureé
1 tablespoon lime juice
1/2 cup sugar
15g (1/2oz) powdered gelatine
1 cup cream
1/4 cup warm water

Whip cream, add pureé, sugar and
lime juice. Dissolve gelatine in
warm water and add to mixture.
Whip until creamy. Pour into ring
mould and allow to set. Unmould
and fill centre of mould with mango
slices and fresh deseeded cherries.
Pawpaws, guavas or any soft fruit
may be used.

Ice Cream & Sherbet

Whipped Cream

Chill heavy cream thoroughly. Whip in a chilled bowl with a chilled beater until cream becomes double in bulk.

Ice Cream Maker

Simple electric ice cream churns can be used to achieve a better quality ice cream with the following recipes. Allow the mixture to become as cold as possible without solidifying. Pour it into the pre-frozen base of the ice cream maker with the motor turning and run it until the ice cream is light and nearly frozen before pouring into a covered container and placing in a freezer to finish it off.

Vanilla Ice Cream

recipe for Custard Sauce or Economical Custard (See page 89)
1 cup evaporated milk or fresh cream
sugar to taste
2 teaspoons vanilla essence

Mix all ingredients together and freeze. Either custard base may be used with other flavourings as a basic recipe.

Guava Ice Cream

About 2 dozen ripe guavas
2 cups milk
2 cups water
sugar to taste

Peel the guavas and cut in half, removing the seeds. Tie the seeds up in a piece of muslin and put them in a saucepan with the water. Bring to the boil and add 1 cup of sugar and the guavas. Boil again until guavas are soft, then take out the bag of seeds and rub the guavas through a sieve or puree in a blender. Add cold milk and sugar to taste, blending well. Allow to cool and freeze.

Coconut Ice Cream

1 large coconut (grated)
or 1 tin of coconut milk
sugar to taste
2 beaten egg whites
recipe for Custard Sauce or Economical Custard (See page 89) using almond essence

Cover the grated coconut with 1 1/2 cups warm water and allow it to stand for 1/2 hour. Then squeeze out the coconut milk, mix it well with the custard and sugar to taste. Fold in beaten egg whites before freezing.

Pineapple, Tangerine, Lime or Orange Sherbet

2 cups water
225g (8oz) castor or granulated sugar
2 egg whites (stiffly beaten)
1 cup fresh or canned pineapple or orange juice
2 tablespoons powdered gelatin

Mix gelatin in a few tablespoons of the cold water. Put the rest of water and sugar in a saucepan. Bring to the boil and remove from the heat when the sugar dissolves, stirring it. Add the gelatin mixture and stir well. Cool and add fruit juice, then fold in beaten egg whites. Freeze. Lime sherbet may be made similarly using: 1/2 cup fresh lime juice, 1/2 cup water, 1 cup pineapple juice.

Pawpaw Water Ice

Pawpaw
Sugar
Water
lime or orange juice

Crush some pawpaw to make a pulp. Add a little water to make the mixture the consistency of thick cream; add sugar to taste and flavour with the fruit juice. Freeze.

Raisin Bread Pudding

Vanilla Pudding

1/3 cup sugar
2 1/2 cups milk or single cream
3 tablespoons cornstarch
1 1/2 teaspoons vanilla
1/4 teaspoon salt

Mix sugar, cornstarch and salt; gradually blend in milk. Cook over medium heat, stirring constantly, till mixture thickens. Cook for 2 or 3 minutes more. Add vanilla. Pour into 5 or 6 individual moulds and chill; or pour into large mould and chill until firm. Unmould and serve with Chocolate Sauce.

Mango Brown Betty

2 cups under ripe mango slices
3 tablespoons butter
3/4 cup brown sugar
2/3 cup breadcrumbs
3 tablespoons water (if necessary)
1/2 teaspoon nutmeg

Melt fat and add breadcrumbs and nutmeg. Place layer of buttered crumbs in oiled baking dish. Add layer of mangoes. Sprinkle with sugar and cinnamon. Finish with crumbs on top layer. Bake for 1 hour in a moderate oven.

Raisin Bread Pudding

2 1/4 cups milk
1/2 teaspoon cinnamon (spice)
2 slightly beaten eggs
1 teaspoon vanilla
2 cups stale bread cut in 2.5cm (1in) cubes (buttered)
1/4 teaspoon salt
1/2 cup seedless raisins
1/2 cup brown sugar

Combine milk and eggs; pour over bread cubes. Stir in remaining ingredients. Pour mixture in a round baking dish. Place in shallow pan on oven rack; pour hot water around it 2.5cm (1in) deep. Bake in a moderate oven for about 45 minutes or till knife inserted halfway between centre and outside comes out clean.

Rum Sauce

100g (4oz) butter
200g (8oz) soft brown sugar
1 sherry glass rum

Beat the butter to a cream and beat in the sugar. When light and creamy, add the rum gradually. Transfer to a serving dish and chill thoroughly before using.

Economical Custard Sauce (Using Cornflour)

25g (1oz) cornstarch
piece of lemon rind
600ml (1 pint) milk
1/2 teaspoon essence
1 1/2 tablespoons sugar

Blend the cornflour with a little of the cold milk. Boil the rest of the milk with the thinly cut lemon rind if used. Remove rind and stir the boiling liquid into the blended cornflour. Rinse the pan and return the sauce to it. Bring to boiling point and boil for 3 minutes. Sweeten and flavour the sauce, unless lemon rind has been used for flavouring.

Hard Sauce

75g (3oz) butter
1 teaspoon - 1 tablespoon rum
150g (6oz) icing sugar or
110g (4 1/2oz) icing sugar and
25g (1oz) ground almonds
1 whipped egg white (optional)

Cream the butter till soft. Sift the icing sugar and cream it with the butter till white and light in texture. Mix in the almonds if used. Work the rum carefully into the mixture. Fold the stiffly-whipped egg white into the sauce. Serve with Christmas or steamed puddings.

Waffles

Pancake Batter

2 cups flour
2 cups milk
2 tablespoons melted margarine
2 eggs
2 tablespoons sugar
fat for greasing pan
1/2 teaspoon salt

Sift flour and salt in bowl. Add sugar and blend. Beat eggs and essence in another bowl and stir in milk. Slowly add dry ingredients to the liquid mixture beating well. Pour the batter into a jug and allow it to stand for an hour or so before cooking. When ready, melt a small bit of fat in a small omelette pan over the heat, and drain it off when it becomes very hot. Start to fry pancakes by pouring in some batter and allowing it to spread over the pan. Cook for about two minutes loosening edges with a spatula. When bubbles appear on the surface turn or toss the pancake, cooking until pale brown. Sprinkle with lime juice and sugar or cinnamon and sugar. Roll and keep hot. Continue, until all the batter is used up but without adding any more fat to the pan. This quantity makes about 18 pancakes.

For Orange Pancakes, peel oranges thickly and remove fruit sections; cut them into thin slices, dredge with sugar and roll between the pancakes. Serve warm.

For Savoury Pancakes, put a little fish or cheese mixture on each pancake, roll and serve.

Tossing the pancake to turn it over in the pan is an art which has been unsuccessfully tried by many cooks. It adds interest to the making of pancakes and can be done with a little practice. When the under side of the pancake is finished, tip the pan downwards slightly and gently shake the pancake a little over the edge of the pan; then with a quick upward jerk of the pan, flip it over on the uncooked side and finish cooking.

Waffles

2 cups sifted flour
1 1/4 cups milk
3 teaspoons baking powder
1/2 cup melted shortening
1/2 teaspoon salt
2 stiffly beaten egg whites
2 beaten egg yolks

Sift together dry ingredients. Combine egg yolks and milk; stir into dry ingredients. Stir in shortening. Lightly fold in egg whites. Bake in pre-heated electric waffle maker. Makes about 8 waffles.

Coffee and Tea Occasions

Afternoon tea parties may be formal or informal. Small parties at home are often informal, but larger club room parties, held in honour of special guests, may be formal. In either case, the host or hostess will want to prepare a variety of sandwiches, cakes and snacks.

Whether for a formal meeting or a relaxing mid morning get together with friends, coffee served with a variety of cakes and cookies provide enjoyable sustanance. Home baked items that go well with coffee also make popular gifts to friends or to take into the office to serve at coffee breaks.

Rita Springer's Caribbean Cookbook

Rock Buns

Scones (Basic Recipe)

2 cups flour
1/2 teaspoon salt
4 teaspoons baking powder
2 teaspoons sugar
2/3 cup milk
4 tablespoons shortening

Sift together flour, baking powder, salt and sugar. Cut in shortening until mixture resembles coarse crumbs. Add cold milk all at once. Stir quickly with a fork until dough leaves the bowl cleanly. Turn dough (which should be soft but not sticky) on to a lightly floured board. Toss lightly to make dough into a ball, and roll out 1.5cm (1/2in) thick. Cut with biscuit cutter, brush with milk or egg and bake in a hot oven for 15-20 minutes.

For Tea Scones, add 2 tablespoons sugar, 1 beaten egg, 1/2 teaspoon vanilla essence, using 1/2 cup milk. For Girdle Scones, use basic recipe cutting dough 6mm (1/4in) thick and bake on both sides on a greased hot baking iron (tawa), electric hot plate or heavy frying pan.
Add rind to fruit juices and let stand for 15 minutes. Strain. Add gradually to egg yolk. Stir in sugar until of very thick consistency. Beat until very smooth.

Rock Buns

225g (8oz) flour
1 teaspoon baking powder
75g (3oz) butter
1 egg
100g (4oz) granulated sugar
1 teaspoon vanilla essence or lemon
100g (4oz) raisins or
1 cup grated coconut plus 2oz flour

Rub together butter and sugar with fork. Add beaten egg and essence. Stir in flour, baking powder and raisins or coconut. Roll into buns and bake in moderate oven.

Butter Sponge

Use any number of eggs, their weight in granulated sugar, butter and flour. Cream butter and sugar, add well-beaten egg yolks with a little vanilla essence, grated lime rind and a little water. Mix in sifted flour lightly. Fold in egg whites last. Bake in moderate oven. Spread over with icing and decorate with peanuts or cherries.

Two-egg Cake

3/4 cup shortening
2 1/4 cups sifted cake flour
1 1/4 cups sugar (granulated)
2 1/2 teaspoons baking powder
1 teaspoon vanilla
1 teaspoon salt
2 eggs
1 cup milk

Cream shortening to soften. Gradually add sugar and cream thoroughly. Add vanilla. Add eggs one at a time, beating well after each. Sift flour with baking powder and salt; add to creamed mixture alternately with milk, beating after each addition. Bake in moderate oven 190°C, 375°F or Gas 5 for about 45 minutes.

This is a good basic recipe for Plain or Fruit Cake. Add 1 cup raisins or mixed fruit or 1/2 cup floured glace cherries. Bake in square shallow pans and cut in pieces. Use for small tea cakes also. Top with glace icing or fluffy frosting and decorate.

Chocolate Cake

Chocolate Cake

1 cup shortening
2 cups sugar
2 teaspoons vanilla
2 2.5cm (1oz) squares unsweetened chocolate, melted or
6 tablespoons cocoa
5 eggs
2 1/4 cups sifted flour
1 teaspoon soda
1 teaspoon salt
1 cup sour milk or buttermilk

Stir shortening to soften. Gradually add sugar, creaming till light and fluffy. Blend in vanilla and cooled chocolate. Add eggs, one at a time, beating well after each.
Sift together flour, soda and salt; add to creamed mixture alternately with milk, beating after each addition. Bake in moderate oven for 20 to 25 minutes. When cold, ice with Chocolate Icing.

Chocolate Icing

50g (2oz) cocoa
200g (8oz) icing sugar
3-4 tablespoons warm water

Blend sieved icing sugar with cocoa. Mix well with water until smooth.

Glacé Icing

200g (8oz) icing sugar
2 tablespoons warm water
flavouring (optional)
colouring (optional)

Roll lumps out of sugar. Sieve in a bowl and place over hot water. Add warm water gradually. Beat until icing is smooth and warm. Remove from heat. Add flavouring and colouring gradually. The icing should coat the back of the spoon. Cool and use on cakes and sweet bread.

Fluffy Frosting

1 cup sugar
dash of salt
1/3 cup water
1 egg white
1/4 teaspoon cream of tartar
1/4 teaspoon vanilla

Bring sugar, water, cream of tartar, and salt to boil; cook until sugar dissolves.
Slowly add to unbeaten egg white, beating constantly with electric or rotary beater until it is of spreading consistency. Add vanilla.

Sponge Cake

6 egg yolks
1/4 teaspoon salt
1/2 cup cold water
1/2 teaspoon vanilla
1 1/2 cups flour
1 1/2 cups sugar
3/4 teaspoon cream of tartar
1 teaspoon orange or lemon juice

Beat egg yolks till thick and lemon-coloured; add water; continue beating till very thick. Gradually beat in sugar, then vanilla and orange extract. Sift flour with salt three times; fold into egg-yolk mixture a little at a time.
Beat egg whites with cream of tartar till stiff peaks form. Fold into first mixture, turning bowl gradually. Bake in greased and lightly floured pan in slow oven for about 1 hour. Invert pan to cool.

Crust for Sponge Cake

1 1/4 tablespoons sugar
1 tablespoon flour

Mix sugar and flour together. Dust insides of greased pans and sprinkle on top of cake before baking, in tube or round pans.

Jam or Swiss Roll

Jam or Swiss Roll

1 1/2 cups flour
4 eggs
2 teaspoons baking powder
1 1/2 cups castor sugar
1/4 teaspoon salt
1 1/2 teaspoons vanilla
2/3 cup milk
2 tablespoons margarine
jam for spreading

Sift dry ingredients. Heat milk and melt margarine in it. Beat egg in bowl until frothy. Gradually add sugar continuing to beat until light. Add essence. Fold in dry ingredients. Fold in liquid last until just blended. Pour thinly into prepared shallow pan greased and then lined with greaseproof paper. Bake in hot oven for 8-10 minutes.

To roll: Spread a tea towel on table. Cover with a sheet of greaseproof paper liberally sprinkled with castor sugar. Trim 1/4 inch from edges all round cake. Turn cake on to sugared paper, quickly peel off greaseproof paper, spread quickly with warmed jam or jelly, roll up tightly with aid of paper, and leave to cool wrapped in paper and cloth to hold its shape. Butter icing may be used to spread instead of jam. When cold, slice and serve.

For Lady Fingers, use same mixture, fill greased Lady Finger pans 2/3 full, sprinkle top with sugar and flour and bake.

Coffee Cake

100g (4oz) butter or margarine
1 teaspoon baking powder
100g (4oz) castor sugar
2 teaspoons instant coffee
2 eggs
3 tablespoons milk
200g (8oz) plain flour

Cream the fat and sugar until very light and add the eggs one at a time with a dessertspoon of flour. Beat well. Sift the flour, baking powder and coffee and fold lightly into the mixture with the milk. Pour into greased cake-tin and spread evenly. Bake in a fairly hot oven for 35-40 minutes until firm. Cool. Use Coffee Icing (see Glace Icing) and top with peanut halves.

Marble Cake

150g (6oz) sugar
1/2 cup milk
200g (8oz) plain flour
1 teaspoon lime juice
1 1/2 teaspoons baking powder
grated lime peel
1 1/2 dessertspoons cocoa
cochineal (red colouring)
100g (4oz) butter or margarine
vanilla essence
2 eggs

Cream the butter or margarine and sugar and add the eggs alternately with the milk. Sift in together the flour and baking powder and mix well. Divide the mixture into 3 parts. Flavour one part with the cocoa, one with a little grated lime peel and the third part with vanilla essence and a few drops of cochineal. Grease a cake pan and drop in alternate spoonfuls of the 3 mixtures until all is used. Bake in a moderate oven.

Cornmeal Pone

Cornmeal Pone

100g (1/4lb) grated pumpkin
1/2 cup flour
2 cups grated coconut
2 tablespoons shortening
1/2 cup sugar
1 teaspoon spice
1 cup cornmeal
2oz raisins
1/2 teaspoon salt
milk or water to mix

Mix together pumpkin and coconut with dry ingredients. Melt shortening and add. Mix in liquid last. Bake in a greased shallow pan in a moderate oven.

Coconut Bread

4 cups flour
2 cups grated coconut
100g (1/4lb) shortening
1 teaspoon vanilla essence
3/4 cup milk and coconut water
2 teaspoons baking powder
150g (6oz) sugar
150g (6oz) raisins (optional)
1 egg
1/2 teaspoon salt

Sift dry ingredients. Add sugar, then beaten egg with milk, melted shortening and essence. Stir in grated coconut, raisins (floured) if used. Blend ingredients well. Knead slightly on floured board. Shape into loaves and put in greased loaf pan, filling only two thirds of each pan. Dust with fine sugar. Bake in moderate oven. Makes 2 loaves. For heavier Coconut Bread, use only 1 teaspoon baking powder, and 1/2 cup milk. Knead well on board, using extra flour, until dough is very firm. Shape into loaves. Score the tops, and brush with sugar and water. Bake in a moderate oven for about 1 hour.

Gingerbread

1/2 cup shortening
2 teaspoons ginger (powdered or freshly grated)
1 cup brown sugar
1 teaspoon baking powder
2 eggs
1 teaspoon baking soda
1/2 cup cane syrup or molasses
2 cups flour
1/2 teaspoon salt
2/3 cup hot water
1/2 teaspoon spice
1/2 teaspoon nutmeg

Grease and line a shallow tin with waxed paper. Sift dry ingredients. Warm sugar, fat and syrup gently, and add hot water. Add beaten eggs. Combine liquids with dry ingredients and beat thoroughly. Pour thick batter in pans and bake in a slow oven (170°C, 325°F or Gas 3) for about 1 hour.

108

Preserves and Candies

Most Caribbean fruits and vegetables are very suitable for making jam, jellies and preserves. The citrus fruits make good marmalade. It is very satisfying to grow fruit in your garden and use up any surplus by preserving it.

Bear in mind that the more acid fruit make better jams and jellies. They should be picked firm and slightly under-ripe for best flavour and the maximum pectin, which is a substance which allows jam or jelly to set after cooking. If the fruit is not very acid, use a tablespoon of lemon or lime juice per pound of fruit.

Use 1 lb of granulated sugar to 1 lb of fruit when making jellies and about 3/4 lb sugar to 1 lb of fruit for jam. Use a little more if the fruit is very acid. Cook fruit until tender, then add sugar. Simmer until sugar is dissolved, then boil briskly. Stir it often but do not stir unnecessarily while boiling, or the mixture will be cloudy. Use a wooden spoon for stirring. Do not fill pans more than half full when making jams and jellies. Cut fruit into smaller pieces for making jelly. Just cover with water, cook slowly until fruit is very tender, 1 hour or more. Pour into a jelly bag and allow liquid to drip through for several hours or overnight, so that jelly will be clear.

To test when jam is set, remove the pan from the heat. put a little jam on a saucer and let it cool. The surface will wrinkel when pushed with the finger. Test jelly by putting it in a saucer of cold water. If it remains in a soft ball without disintegrating, the jelly is finished. If using a thermometer, the temperature should be 220 F. To sterilize jars for bottling, either put them in cold water and boil for 15 minutes or a cold oven and heat gradually. Sterilize them just before ready for use. Fill jars 1/4" from the top, wipe with a clean damp cloth, cover with a round of waxed paper and put on a tightly fitting metal cover. Store in well ventilated cupboards.

Rita Springer's Caribbean Cookbook

A typical Bajan Shop sweet display case

Orange or Tangerine Marmalade

6 oranges or tangerines
1/2 cup lime juice
Granulated sugar
Water

Wash, fruit. Cut in quarters and remove seeds. Measure fruit pulp. Add 3 cups of water to 1 cup of pulp. Bring to the boil and cook about 1/2 hour. Let it stand overnight. Measure 1 cup liquid to 1 cup sugar and 2 tablespoons lime or lemon juice. Bring fruit mixture to the boil. Add sugar and stir utíl dissolved. Boil rapidly, stirring occasionally until mixture jells in cold water or, if using a candy thermometer, it should register 220F. Allow it to cool and pour into sterlized fars. Seal at once.

Pineapple Jam

2 cups grated pineapple
1 cup water
1 1/2 cups granulated sugar
2 teaspoons lime juice

Cook pineapple with water slowly until soft. Add sugar and lime juice; stir well. Cook until thick and set. Cool and bottle.

Guava Jelly

Guavas (under ripe)
Lime juice
Granulated sugar
Water

To every pound of guavas use a pound of granulated sugar. Wash, peel guavas, cut in halves and put in a saucepan. Cover with water. Boil until guavas are soft. Strain through a colander and then through fine muslin. Measure the juice and use 1 cup sugar to 1 cup juice. Heat juice, add sugar and dissolve before it boils. Add 1/2 teaspoon lime juice per cup liquid. Boil briskly removing gum with wooden spoon, until mixture jells. Test on saucer, bottle and cover.

Peanut Brittle

2 cups sugar
1/4 teaspoon cream of tartar
1/2 cup water
1/4 teaspoon salt
1 cup chopped peanuts
1/4 teaspoon bicarbonate of soda
2 tablespoons butter

Mix sugar, nuts, cream of tartar and water and boil to the 'large crack' stage (156°C or 312°F). Remove from heat and add salt, soda and butter. Pour on to a greased pan and when cold, break into pieces.

Ginger Squares

2 cups granulated sugar
15g (1/2oz) grated green ginger
1/4 cup water
1 teaspoon lime juice
1 teaspoon butter

Boil sugar, water and ginger until syrup makes a firm ball in water. When tested, remove from heat, add lime juice and butter. Beat well and when very thick pour into a wet shallow tin. Cut into squares when firm.

Chocolate Fudge, Peanut Brittle,
Guava Cheese & Coconut Sugar Cakes

Making Fudge

The first time I made fudge the recipe was given to me by a school friend, but when I thought it should have been cooked and I was ready to pour it on to the pan, I was faced with a dark mass of brown stuff sticking to the saucepan. Of course I did not have a candy thermometer at the time, and had not yet learned of the testing method (see recipe). I was told afterwards that at a certain point you have to allow the mixture to cool and then beat it to a dropping consistency, then pour it into a second pan and allow it to set. However, afterwards I invested in a candy thermometer and have had better results ever since when making it by the right recipe. It is important to follow the correct recipe. I have found that out in many instances, otherwise you waste ingredients all the time. Always read and follow a recipe carefully. Be very careful about oven temperatures. Many a cake may be underdone or burnt by a misunderstanding of your oven temperature. Understand clearly the meaning of low, medium and high, check your oven and find out how it relates to those given in the recipes. Ovens sometimes vary.

Chocolate Fudge

2 cups sugar
2 tablespoons cocoa
1 teaspoon vanilla
2 tablespoons butter
1 cup milk

Combine sugar, cocoa and milk, and place over medium heat. Stir steadily until mixture begins to boil, lower heat and continue to cook gently, stirring occasionally. Test by dropping a little into cold water; if it makes a firm ball between the fingers, the fudge is ready. Remove from heat. Add vanilla and butter, beat with wooden spoon until very creamy and beginning to set. Pour into a buttered tin and cut into squares when cool.

Guava Cheese

very ripe guavas
sugar

Peel and grate the guavas or cut them up and whiz them in a food processor. Rub through a coarse net or a sieve. Use 1 cup sugar to every cup of guava pulp. Boil until very thick and the mixture leaves the side of the pan, stirring occassionally while cooking. Test in cold water. Pour into a wet shallow tin about 1/2 inch thick. Cut in squares. When cool, dredge with caster sugar

Coconut Sugar Cake or Coconut Ice

2 cups light crystal or granulated sugar
1/2 teaspoon vanilla essence
1/2 cup water
1 cup grated coconut

Boil sugar and water together until syrupy. Test a few drops in saucer with cold water; when it forms a soft ball, remove from heat. Cool a little, then beat mixture until very thick and it begins to crystallize. Stir in essence and coconut; blend well and pour into a greased shallow pan 20 x 20 x 2.5cm (8 x 8 x 1in). Mixture may be divided into half and coloured pink, using a few drops of red dye, or a pink layer may be placed on a white layer to make a two-colour cake. Cut in 5cm (2in) squares. Work quickly and do not overbeat mixture.

Cooling Thirst Quenchers & Cocktail Eats

What can be most refreshing after a hot morning's shopping, an energetic game or a long swim in the sea? A cold icy drink is always the popular choice. In the Caribbean there is a wide variety of local beverages made chiefly from common garden fruits with simple flavourings which are much more delectable, nourishing and economical than the more expensive imported varieties.

As snacks between meals, or served with meals, hosts and visitors alike never cease to enjoy our Caribbean citrus squashes, fruit punches, chilled coconut water, etc. Most home-made drinks take some time to prepare but many will agree that the effort is worth the praise received from those who enjoy them.

Lemonade, the commonest and perhaps most refreshing drink, is made from fresh garden limes, rarely from lemons, as these when locally grown tend to be coarse skinned, seedy and not as juicy and pleasantly flavoured as the yellow Mediterranean species.

Rita Springer's Caribbean Cookbook

Fruit Drinks

Lemonade

Juice of 2-3 large fresh green limes
(strained) (about 1/2 cup)
1/2 teaspoon aromatic bitters
(optional to make a Bentley)
4 cups water
1 lime rind
1 cup granulated sugar

Stir sugar with lime rind in water
until sugar dissolves, add lime juice
and bitters and stir well. Serve at
once in glasses with cracked ice.

Mango Drink

2 medium sized ripe mangos
sugar to taste
1 teaspoon grated ginger or
1 or 2 fresh limes

Slice, peel and crush the mangos. To
every cup of crushed fruit add 1 cup
water, stir thoroughly and strain.
Sweeten to taste and chill or add
cracked ice.
A small bit of ginger, grated, or a
dessertspoon of juice from fresh
green limes will improve the
flavour.
Paw Paw Drink may be made
similarly.

Guava Drink

1/4 teaspoon nutmeg
1 1/2 cups water
2 cups guava puree (fresh ripe)
1/4 teaspoon salt
1 cup sugar

Combine all ingredients. Strain
and chill thoroughly. Serve with
cracked ice. Ginger ale may be
added at the last for variation.

Ginger Beer

100g (1/4lb) green ginger
1 gallon water
1 large green lime
900g (2lb) granulated sugar

Scrape ginger, wash and pound it.
Put it in a large bowl and pour
boiling water over. Stir in the sugar
until dissolved. Peel the lime and
add both lime and rind to the
liquid. Cool and pour in a glass or
earthenware jar. Cover and let it
stand for 6 days, stirring with a
wooden spoon every other day.
When ripe, strain, pour off into
bottles which may be placed in the
refrigerator to chill. Bottles may be
kept at room temperature and
allowed to ripen for a further 2 or 3
days before using.

Mauby

50g (2oz) mauby bark
large piece cinnamon (spice)
12 cupswater
few cloves
piece of mace
piece dried orange peel
brown sugar (about 900g or 2lb)

Boil mauby bark in water (about 4 cups)
with spice, cloves, mace and orange peel
until liquid is very bitter (about 1/2
hour). Strain it off, add the rest of the
water and sugar until very sweet. Bottle
the cooled liquid, leaving neck of bottle
unfilled for froth. Cover and leave for 3
days. Serve very cold.

Tamarind Drink

450g (1lb) shelled tamarinds
4 cups hot water
2 cups brown sugar (or more)
grated nutmeg

Soak tamarinds in hot water for 1
hour and scrape off pulp with a
spoon. Add sugar, stir well and
strain off liquid. Serve very cold
with grated nutmeg. Aerated soda
water may be added to make a more
refreshing drink.

Stuffed Eggs

Cheese Dip

2 cups grated Cheddar cheese
1 tablespoon milk
75g (3oz) cream cheese
1 tablespoon minced onion
salt and pepper to taste

Blend well together and use on toast
or small crackers.

Stuffed Eggs

Cook some eggs until hard-boiled
(15 minutes). Place in cold water for
1/2 hour. Then shell eggs and divide
in halves or quarters. Pick out yolks,
crush them and mix with enough
butter and salad cream to make a
paste, add salt, white pepper and
mix well. Pipe mixture into egg
white pieces or refill with a knife.
Garnish with parsley and pieces of
sweet pepper.

Sandwiches

Always use sandwich bread for best
results when cutting, rolling and
spreading. Trim off crusts. Spread
filling as desired between 2 slices of
bread, and cut in 4 squares or
triangles.
Experiment with filling mixtures,
making them tasty. Cover
sandwiches with a damp towel or
aluminium foil while working and
chill to keep them fresh before
serving.
Use brown or white bread
preferably one-day old and make
different shapes for variety.
Open sandwiches may be made
from 6mm (1/4in) thick bread, cut in
attractive shapes with biscuit cutters
and spread with butter, cream
cheese, peanut butter or salad cream
with cucumber, tomato, olives,
salami, ham, smoked fish, fish roe
and meat slices and garnish with
parsley, watercress, sweet pepper
slices etc.

Tomato-cheese Filling

2 large tomatoes
1 large onion
50g (2oz) cheese
1 teaspoon chopped parsley
2 tablespoons butter
pepper and salt to taste
1 beaten egg
breadcrumbs

Mix together crushed tomato,
chopped onion, salt and pepper and
chopped parsley. Add butter and
beaten egg. Mix well. Cook in
saucepan over heat until egg is
cooked. Take off and stir in grated
cheese and sufficient breadcrumbs
to make a smooth paste. Use for
sandwiches, bouchées, and on toast.

Sardine and Egg Filling

1 tin sardines
2 hard boiled eggs
1 tablespoon butter
pepper and salt to taste
1 teaspoon lime juice
1 teaspoon chopped parsley

Crush sardines and eggs with
butter. Add pepper and salt to taste,
then lime juice and chopped parsley.
Blend well. Fish may be substituted
for sardines.

Cheese Biscuits & Straws

Curried Salt Fish Cakes

1 1/2 cups prepared salt fish
1 tablespoon minced onion and
herbs
1/2 cup mashed yam or potato
1 egg
2 tablespoons flour
salt and pepper to taste
1 tablespoon curry powder
breadcrumbs and flour or seasoned
flour
oil for frying
1 tablespoon butter

Shred fish finely. Mix in dry
ingredients, mashed potato and
beaten egg. Make into small balls,
roll in seasoned flour or
breadcrumbs and flour. Allow to
stand for about 15 minutes. Fry in
deep fat until golden brown. Serve
hot on toothpicks. Dip in cocktail
sauce.

Cocktail Sauce

1/2 cup tomato sauce
1 teaspoon salt
1 teaspoon Worcestershire sauce
1/2 teaspoon white pepper
1 tablespoon minced onion
1 tablespoon lime juice
1 teaspoon paprika

Blend well together and use for fish
and seafood snacks.

Cheese Biscuits & Straws

100g (4oz) flour
1/2 teaspoon cayenne pepper
1/4 teaspoon salt
100g (4oz) grated cheese
75g (3oz) margarine
1 egg yolk
iced water

Mix flour, grated cheese, salt and
pepper together. Rub in margarine
and mix to a smooth paste with yolk
of egg. This can be done most easily
in a food processor. Pipe out with
cookie press or forcing bag or cut
into straws or thin strips and twist.
For biscuits, use 40g (1 1/2oz)
margarine, 50g (2oz) cheese and a
little beaten yolk to make a stiff
rolling dough. Cut strips 6cm x 1 cm
(2 1/2in x 1/2in) and bake in a
moderate oven for about 20
minutes.

Press Cookies

2 cups flour
1 egg
100g (4oz) margarine or butter
1 teaspoon baking powder
100g (4oz) sugar
cherries to decorate
1 teaspoon vanilla

Cream together margarine and
sugar. Add beaten egg and essence
and mix in flour sifted with baking
powder. Mix to a soft dough. Place
dough in cookie press or forcing
bag and pipe into shapes, adding
dough to the press until all is used
up. Decorate with cherries or nuts.

Meat Patties can also be
folded and sealed at the side
Jamaican style

Meat Patties

few sprigs thyme and marjoram
100g (4oz) minced beef
1 tablespoon butter
100g (4oz) minced pork
1/2 teaspoon Worcestershire Sauce
25g (1oz) bacon
2 tablespoons flour
piece of red pepper
1/2 cup stock
1 onion

200g (8oz) rich short crust
beaten egg

Sauté bacon, minced beef and pork with salt to taste in a little oil until it is cooked. Cool and whiz in a food processor with the pepper and other herbs. Make a binding sauce by melting the margarine in the saucepan, add the flour, then the stock slowly until it is smooth. Add this to the minced mixture and stir in the Worcestershire Sauce making a paste. Cut the rolled dough in 5cm (2in) rounds with a pastry cutter and place a small teaspoon of the mixture on each round. Cover with another round of dough, damping the inner edges. Press the edges together with a fork, and with a skewer, make a hole in the centre of each patty on the top and brush with beaten egg. When finished, bake the patties in a greased shallow baking tin in a hot oven for about 20 minutes or until brown.

Rich Short Crust Pastry

225g (8 oz) flour
75g (3oz) lard
75g (3oz) margarine
1/3 cup iced water & a little lime juice
1/2 teaspoon salt
1/2 teaspoon sugar (for sweet dishes)
1 teaspoon dry hot mustard (for savoury dishes)

Sift dry ingredients in a bowl and cut in the fat lightly with two knives or a pastry fork until the mixture resembles breadcrumbs. This can be done very easily and quickly in a food processor the fat must be very cold. Place mixture in a bowl and add the water gradually, tossing the mixture with a fork until a ball is formed which does not stick to the bowl. Wrap in waxed paper and place in the fridge for an hour before working with it. Roll out 1/8 inch thick to make patties and pie crusts. This quantity makes a double 9-10-inch pie or two single shells.

Bouchées

For making bouchées, roll out some rich short pastry very thinly. Cut in rounds 5cm (2in) in diameter and fit neatly into special boucheé tins. Prick dough in the tins and bake until crisp in a moderate oven. Any sandwich fillings may be used. Garnish as desired.

Tips For Making Pastry

Many good cooks are timid about making pastry admitting that it is one of their weaknesses. If, however, a few basic facts are clearly understood, a little practice will make perfect.
1. Use cold ingredients and utensils.
2. Handle as little as possible.
3. Lift the flour while cutting the fat into the flour to introduce cold air into the mixture.
4. Use iced cold water for mixing.
5. A little lemon or lime juice also helps to lighten the mixture.
6. Dough should be pliable but not sticky.
7. Dough should not be too crumbly.
8. Wrap the pastry and chill for an hour before rolling it out.
9. Roll thinly and quickly with a rolling pin away from the body, lifting it between strokes .
10. Use just enough flour while rolling. Always turn the dough before cutting in shapes.
11. Pastry needs a very hot oven for baking to expand the dough and so make it light.

Short pastry is a good everyday pastry and, if well made, is adequate for most requirements. For a less rich short pastry use 2 oz less fat and omit the lime juice.
For quiches add 50g (2 oz) grated cheese to the flour.

Rita Springer's Caribbean Cookbook

126

Traditional Dishes of The Caribbean

In the islands and regions of the vast Caribbean area, the climate and food crops may range between tropical and sub tropical, but from the early sixteenth century, when West Africans were brought over as slaves by traders from some of the European countries, food crops of all kinds were interchanged between territories and grown and produced as required, and according to the suitability of the soil, rainfall, etc. Although food produced and dishes are similar throughout the area, methods of cooking vary according to the original influences. In the rural communities of each island unique traditional dishes evolved.

After the abolition of slavery in the early nineteenth century, the Africans were refusing to work on the plantations in the larger islands. Chinese and Indian emigrants were then encouraged to do this work with limited success. They, however, remained and opened laundries, restaurants and provision shops. Asians make a large percentage of the populations of Guyana, Trinidad and Jamaica and their food forms an integral part of the regions cuisine.

Rita Springer's Caribbean Cookbook

Ackee & Salt Fish

Jerk Pork

This is a speciality of Portland, Port Antonio. A young pig about 13.5kg (30 lb) in weight, cleaned and prepared for cooking, is used for 'jerking'. A mixture of blood, pepper, pimento seeds, escallion, minced onions and salt, is rubbed inside the belly cavity. A stand made of green pimento or other sticks, or 'pata' is fixed up over a coal fire and the pig is placed on the stand. The fat is allowed to fall in the fire. Men who prepare and sell this meat are known as 'jerk men'. They sell this delicacy in the market square and heat the meat in an oven at one of the local bakeries.
This jerk pork often lasts for several weeks.

Rice and Peas

1 cup red beans
1 tin coconut milk
2 blades chives
2 rashers bacon
salt to taste
2 cups rice
1 sweet pepper
piece of red hot pepper
1 clove garlic

Cook beans in coconut milk and 1 cup water covered until tender. Add all other ingredients except rice and cook for 10 minutes. Add washed rice and 3 cups water. Cook over a low heat covered, until the grains are soft. Garnish with slices of sweet pepper.

Ackee and Salt Fish

2 dozen ackees or one tin
2 medium onions
450g (1lb) salt fish
few blades of escallion
piece of hot pepper
1/2 green pepper
2 tablespoons butter

Boil fish after soaking in cold water to remove salt. Flake. Remove ackees from pods, seeds and red centre. Wash and put into cold water; boil for 15 minutes. When cooked, place them over flaked fish and serve hot with the following dressing: Chop onions and escallion finely. Toss lightly in 2 tablespoons butter with hot pepper. Garnish with pieces of green pepper.

Pepper Pot Soup

1 bunch of Indian kale
1 bunch of callaloo
1 lb fresh beef
1/2 lb salt beef
8 cups water
few shrimps or a crab
2 cocoes
1 dozen okras
seasoning (bunch of mixed herbs)

Boil the vegetables and meat till tender, then remove the meat and blend up the greens. Return to the pot and add seasonings. Simmer. Cut okras in rings and fry lightly in butter. Add to soup 10 minutes before serving.

Green Corn Dumplings

2 cups freshly grated corn
2 cups flour
milk or water
3-4 oz beef suet or lard
1 tablespoon salt

Remove husks and clean rip corn. Grate on a sharp grater. Add flour and salt sifted. Mix in shredded suet or lard. Pour in milk or water and mix to mellow dough. Shape into dumpliongs and cook in boiling water for 20 minutes.

Pudding & Souse

Cou-Cou

2 cups corn meal (sifted)
1 tablespoon salt or to taste
12 okras
2 tablespoons butter
6 cups water or more

Wash okras, cut off stems, slice into rings and boil with half the water and salt for about 10 minutes. Add the rest of the water and salt to the sifted corn meal and mix well. Remove saucepan from heat and stir in the corn meal mixture until well blended. Return saucepan to stove and cook mixture stirring ingredients with a wooden spatula over medium heat. When mixture becomes stiff and smooth, and breaks away from saucepan cleanly at bottom, it is finished. Put into a dish immediately and spread liberally with butter. Serve with Steamed Flying Fish.

Pudding and Souse

Pudding

Thoroughly clean some of the intestines of a pig (turning skins inside out) with soap and water and then salt water and lime juice. Then soak in a salt water and lime solution for about 1 hour. Grate 900g-1.35kg (2 3lb) of sweet potatoes in a bowl. For Black Pudding, strain some of the pig's blood mixed with water and add minced eschalots, thyme, red pepper, sweet marjoram, 4 tablespoons margarine, salt to taste, 1 tablespoon sugar and 1/2 teaspoon powdered cloves. Add water to make a mixture of loose consistency. Fill the skins (do not pack tightly) with mixture, tie at each end and steam or cook slowly in boiling water until potato is cooked and skins firm. Prick the skins in places when half cooked to expel air and prevent bursting. For White Pudding, blood is not added to ingredients.

Souse

Divide a pig's head in half. Wash, scrape and clean well with a sharp knife. Remove the brain, and boil in salted water until the flesh begins to leave the bones. Plunge immediately into cold salted water to make the flesh crisp, and to cool. Then cut off the meat in slices and put into a large bowl of pickle made from salt water, lime juice, chopped onion, cucumber and a few sliced red peppers. Leave for several hours to steep before using. Garnish with parsley. This is a popular Saturday meal. Pigs' trotters are also cooked and soused.

Conkies

Conkies

It was traditional in Barbados to make conkies on Guy Fawkes Day, 5 November, although the origin of the custom is unknown. Conkie is probably a corruption of the West African word 'kenky' used up to the present day, for a similarly prepared corn meal dish.

2 cups fresh corn flour
100g (4oz) raisins (optional)
1/2 cup flour
325g (3/4lb) brown sugar
325g (3/4lb) pumpkin
1 cup milk
150g (6oz) shortening
1 teaspoon powdered spice
225g (1/2lb) sweet potato
1 teaspoon grated nutmeg
3 cups grated coconut (1 large)
1 teaspoon almond essence
1 teaspoon salt.

Grate coconut, pumpkin and sweet potato. Mix in sugar, liquids and spices. Add raisins and flour last and combine well. Melt shortening before adding with milk, etc. Fold a few tablespoons of the mixture in steamed plaintain leaves cut in squares about 20cm (8in) wide. Steam conkies on a rack over boiling water in a large pot or in a steamer until they are firm and cooked.

Jug-Jug

Jug-Jug is a corruption of the Scottish dish haggis, which was introduced by the Scots who were exiled in Barbados after the Monmouth Rebellion of 1685. The original haggis is a savoury mixture of oatmeal, blended with minced liver, suet, etc., well-seasoned and steamed like a pudding. In cooking jug-jug, whole grain, ground guinea corn flour (millet) is substituted for oatmeal. Okras are sometimes chopped and cooked in this dish This is a very rich dish and is served in a casserole topped with butter. It is traditionally an accompaniement to baked ham at Christmas.

8 cups green peas
2 medium sized onions
1 cup guinea corn flour
3-4 blades eschalot (chives)
225g (1/2lb) salt beef or any other salted meat
1 bunch mixed herbs
100g (1/4lb) fresh pork or chicken
salt and pepper to taste
2 tablespoons butter
about 4 cups water
Boil the pork or chicken in water; add the salt meat cut in pieces and soaked previously to remove the salt; also add the peas and herbs. Cook the mixture until peas are soft. Now strain it off reserving the stock. Mince the meat, peas and seasonings. Cook the guinea corn flour in the stock for about 10 minutes, stirring constantly. Add minced ingredients, stir and cook for about 1/2 hour stirring the mixture until it becomes a fairly stiff consistency. Cover and allow to steam for 5 minutes. Before removing from the heat, stir in some of the butter, then turn mixture out on a dish.

Fowl Down-in-Rice

1 chicken (3-4 lb)
4 cups rice
1/4 lb onions
1 tablespoon salt
8 cups water
2 tablespoons butter
1/2 teaspoon mustard
1/4 lb tomatoes
1 lime
sprigs of fresh thyme and marjoram

Clean and wash chicken with salt and lime. Allow to stand for about 1 hour. Cook chicken in water for 1/2 hour. Wash rice and add to chicken with herbs, pepper and salt to taste. Cook until the rice grains are soft. Serve with a sauce of sliced onions, tomatoes, butter, mustard and lime juice mixed in with 1/2 cup of water and cooked for 5 minutes.

Rita Springer's Caribbean Cookbook

Brule Jol & Bakes

Callaloo

16-20 dasheen or eddoe leaves
1 tablespoon butter
100g (1/4lb) pig's tail or salted meat
8-10 okras
1 large crab or a tin of crab
1 large coconut or a tin of coconut
milk
4 tablespoons cooking oil
a piece green hot pepper
1 lime
1 onion
2 blades chives (eschalot)
sprig of thyme

Wash leaves and break into fine
pieces. Grate coconut. Add 2 cups of
hot water and extract milk. Wash
crab with lime. Extract crab meat
and shred it. Cut up salt meat and
okras. Place ingredients in sauce
pan, cover and leave to boil until
leaves are tender. Swizzle and leave
to simmer until smooth and okra
seeds are pink. Serve with pounded
plaintain (foo foo).

Brule Jol

225g (8oz) salt fish
1 tablespoon salad oil
1 small chopped onion
1 lime
2 medium sized tomatoes
piece of red pepper
1 avocado pear
1/2 teaspoon white pepper

Soak fish overnight to remove salt.
Clean and shred fish. Mix chopped
tomato, onion, pepper and shredded
fish in a bowl. Marinate with olive
oil and lemon juice. Serve with
bakes.

Bakes

1 1/2 cups flour
2 teaspoons sugar
1 teaspoon baking powder
(rounded)
1 tablespoon shortening
1/2 teaspoon salt
1/4 cup water
oil for frying

Sift flour, baking powder and salt.
Rub in fat. Add dry ingredient and
mix to make a soft dough. Knead
lightly, with extra flour if needed.
Break off pieces and roll into balls.
Then flatten to 2cm (1/2in) thick.
Fry or bake on a hot greased tawa at a
medium heat until cooked through.

Paimie

2 cups corn meal
1/4 cup raisins
1/4 cup shortening
salt and black pepper to taste
2 cups grated coconut
225g (1/2lb) fresh or salt meat
1 cup grated pumpkin
1 cup water
1/2 cup flour
plantain leaves

Mix together all ingredients and
blend well. Prepare banana leaves
and cut into 15-20cm (6-8in)
squares. Put 2 tablespoons of
mixture in the centre of each square.
Fold over leaves and tie securely.
Steam for about 3/4 hour.
1 cup of sugar may be substituted
for the pepper and meat to make
Sweet Paimies.

Pepper Pot

Pepper Pot

This dish is an Amerindian speciality and has become one of the national dishes of Guyana. Its chief seasoning ingredient is cassareep, the thick syrupy residue from boiled cassava juice. The juice is extracted by grating the raw cassava, adding water and straining. Cassareep is seasoned with salt, pepper and sugar and is a preservative for meat. Pepper Pot lasts for some time, provided it is boiled up every day. Freshly cooked pieces of meat may be added and simmered in it. No onions, vegetables or starchy foods must be used in it.

1.8kg (4lb) cow heel, stew beef, pork or pig trotters
225g (1/2lb) salt beef or pig's tail
2 tablespoons brown sugar
salt to taste
1/2 cup cassareep
1 or 2 hot peppers
1 stick cinnamon
few cloves

Cut meat into pieces; wash well with salt and water and put to boil well covered. Add cassareep and allow to simmer. When half-done, add other ingredients. Put in peppers with sterns and remove before they burst or they may be put in a muslin bag strung over the side of the saucepan. Keep on boiling until meat is tender and liquid just covers it. Serve hot with boiled rice, Eclipse biscuits or boiled sweet potato.

Garlic Pork

1.8kg (4lb) pork
2 cups vinegar
salt to taste
thyme
fat for frying
100g (1/4lb) garlic
1 lime

Chop the garlic and thyme and mix. Add salt to taste. Wash pork well in lime and salt and cut into small pieces. Parboil pork in water to cover for about 20 minutes. Remove pork from water, dress with seasonings and place in an earthenware bowl or jar. Pour on vinegar to cover pork, and allow to stand for 1-2 days. Remove from jar and fry in deep fat. Serve hot.

Cassava Pone

3 cups dry cassava flour
1 teaspoon salt
100g (1/4lb) shortening
2 cups grated coconut
1 1/2 cups sugar
1 or 2 eggs
3 cups milk and water
1 teaspoon vanilla essence
1/2 teaspoon powdered orange peel
1 1/2 teaspoons mixed spice or rind of 1/2 orange

Mix dry ingredients together. Add melted shortening, milk, beaten eggs and essence. Blend well. Pour mixture into greased shallow tin and bake in a moderate oven for about 1 1/2 hours. Glaze with sugar and water before baking.
Note: When freshly grated cassava is used, decrease the amount of liquid.

Pancake Rolls

Chow Mein

225g (1/2lb) package egg noodles
1/2 cup diced chicken or cooked pork
1/2 cup diced celery
1/2 cup sliced onions
1 scrambled egg, shredded
1 cup chicken broth or water
1/2 cup bean sprouts
1/2 cup cabbage
50g (2oz) mushrooms
1 tablespoon corn starch
2 tablespoons soy sauce
1 tablespoonoil for frying

Fry chicken or pork in fat; add celery, onion and chicken broth. Cover and cook till vegetables are tender. Add bean sprouts, cabbage and mushrooms, and bring to boil. Add noodles boiled for 5 minutes, drained and fried. Mix corn starch with soy sauce and add to hot mixture, stirring. Simmer for 2-3 minutes. Arrange in deep bowl and garnish with scrambled egg.

Fried Rice

4 cups cooked rice
1/2 teaspoon salt
100g (4oz) roast lean pork
50g (2oz) fresh shrimps
50g (2oz) cooked ham
1/4 teaspoon white pepper
1 tablespoon soy sauce
1 egg

Finely chop pork, shrimp and ham. Heat greased pan well, put in cooked ham, lean pork and fresh shrimps and sauté for 3 minutes. Add cooked rice, mix together and fry for 3 minutes again. Add soy sauce, Ve-Tsin powder, salt and pepper. Break egg and stir well into hot mixture. Fry for 2 minutes more and serve.

Pancake Batter

1 cup flour
1/4 teaspoon salt
1 egg
1 cup water

Sift flour and salt. Make a well in centre. Put in egg, add water gradually and stir well to make a creamy batter. Allow it to stand for an hour or so. To fry Pancakes, lightly grease pan and heat. Pour in 2 tablespoons batter and allow it to spread over the pan. Cook pancakes on one side only, and stand on rack on cooked side.

Pancake Rolls

Filling

1/2 cup meat mixture (chicken, ham, pork, etc.)
1 teaspoon soy sauce
1/4 teaspoon grated ginger
2 tablespoons shrimps
salt and sugar to taste
1/2 cup bean sprouts, mushrooms and bamboo shoots
1 tablespoon sherry
1 tablespoon cooking oil
parsley
2 medium onions, chopped

Cut meat into thin pieces. Cut mushroom and bamboo shoots in thin slices. Sauté onion in oil. Add meat, vegetables and shrimps; cook for 2 minutes, stirring. Season to taste, add soy sauce and sherry. Stir well off heat and cool.
To fill, put some filling on one-half of the cooked side, fold the other side over, sealing and pressing the ends together with some of the batter to make a sealed roll. Deep fry the pancakes till pale brown and drain on kitchen paper or bake in a hot oven for 10 minutes. Garnish with parsley.

140

Roti

Sweet and Sour Pork

325g (12oz) lean pork (in 2.5cm
or 1 inch cubes)
1/2 teaspoon ground ginger
1 tablespoon cooking sherry
salt and pepper to taste
groundnut oil for frying
1/2 cup flour
salt to taste

Sauce and Garnish
1 tablespoon cornflour
1/2 cup pickled cucumber
2 tablespoons brown sugar
1/4 cup carrots
2 tablespoons vinegar
1/2 cup shredded pineapple
1/2 cup water
2 tablespoons oil
2 teaspoons soy sauce

Make batter as for Pancake Rolls on
previous page. Rub seasonings and
sherry in pork and fry in shallow fat
until brown. Drain and dredge with
flour. Shake off and coat pork pieces
with batter. Fry in deep fat until
brown. To make the sauce, shred the
pickles, carrots and pineapple slices
and cook in a tablespoon of oil for 5
minutes. Add soy sauce, water, sugar
and vinegar. Simmer for 15 minutes.
Blend cornflour with 2 tablespoons
water and stir in. Salt to taste and
simmer for 5 minutes longer. Pour
the sauce over the pork. Garnish top
with the vegetables.

Roti

2 cups flour
milk to mix
1/4 teaspoon bicarbonate of soda
ghee or oil to brush
1/4 teaspoon salt

Sift flour, soda and salt together.
Add milk to mix stiff dough. Knead
well. Form in 4 or 5 balls. Flour
board and roll out balls very thinly
and apply ghee or oil to surface,
then roll up into a ball. Allow tawa
or hot-plate to heat in the meantime
(3 minutes). Roll out dough again
and place on baking hot-plate. Rub
with oil again and turn frequently.
Remove and clap with both hands
until very pliable. Wrap in towel
and keep warm. Serve with shrimp,
chicken or meat curry.

Curried Chicken

1 chicken (1.35 kg or 3lb)
2 tablespoons flour
2 tablespoons curry powder or
massala ghee or oil for frying
salt and pepper to taste
2 cups water
1 medium onion
few blades chives (eschalot)
1 clove garlic
few garden tomatoes

Clean and cut chicken in joints and
marinate. Crush garlic, burn in oil.
Remove garlic and brown massala
and chicken pieces previously rolled
in flour. Add rest of seasonings and
water. Cover and simmer until
tender. Stir occasionally.

142

Paella

Spanish Rice

6 slices bacon
1 cup finely chopped onion
1/4 cup chopped green pepper
450g (1lb) sliced tomatoes
4 cups water
2 cups rice
1/2 cup chili sauce
salt and pepper to taste
1 teaspoon brown sugar
1 tablespoon vinegar
8 strands of saffron (optional)

Fry bacon until crisp; remove from heat. Sauté onion and green pepper in bacon fat. Add rest of ingredients. Simmer until rice grains are soft. Garnish with pieces of bacon and parsley.

Paella

1 chicken (about 1.1 kg or 2 1/2lb)
1 medium-sized onion
2 cloves garlic (chopped)
2 tablespoons salad or vegetable oil
150g (6oz) shrimp or other shell fish
1 cup peas or white beans (cooked)
a little yellow food colouring
225g (1/2lb) rice
water or stock
1 green sweet pepper
2 large tomatoes
2 tablespoons vinegar
salt and pepper to taste
1 tablespoon wine
8 strands of saffron (optional)

Cut chicken in pieces. Marinate in vinegar and one teaspoon salt. Drain well. Brown lightly in hot oil in a heavy pan over medium heat. Add sliced onion and garlic and stir well. Add rice and when it has absorbed the oil add a little water or stock, stir and allow rice to cook and absorb the liquid until rice is about half-cooked. Then add shell fish,, sliced tomatoes, wine, beans, salt and pepper to taste and a little food colouring to make the mixture a pale yellow colour. Stir well, cover and steam over low heat until rice grains are soft but not sticky. Add green peas 5 minutes before serving. Garnish with slices of green sweet pepper.

Pastelles

3 cups grated green corn or same quantity in corn balls
few capers or sweet pickles
1/2 cup raisins
450g (1lb) minced beef (cooked)
2 medium onions
450g (1lb) minced pork (cooked)
1/4 cup cooking oil
2 large tomatoes
piece of sweet pepper
1 tablespoon vinegar
2 blades chives (eschalot)
1/2 teaspoon black pepper
plantain or banana leaves

Chop all green seasonings finely and mix with meat. Brown in hot oil; add chopped tomatoes, raisins and sweet pepper. Blend well together. Cut plantain leaves in 20cm (8in) squares, clean them with a damp cloth and steam them over hot water to make them pliable. Crush corn and dampen with a little salted water. Butter the leaf squares and spread with the corn mixture. Place 2 tablespoons of the meat mixture on each square leaving a 2.5cm (1in) border. Fold over and tie securely into a parcel, using thread. Steam for about 1 hour.

Sopped Biscuits

Shepherd's Pie

2 cups cooked meat
1 beaten egg
1 medium onion, chopped
salt and pepper to taste
900g (2lb) cooked mashed potatoes
1 cup meat gravy
1 1/2 tablespoons butter

Cut the meat into small pieces. Add gravy, onion, pepper and salt to taste. Put in a buttered oven dish. Mix potatoes with nearly all the butter and egg. Add a little salt to taste, and mix well. Spread the mixture over the meat. Lightly butter the top, stroking with a fork to decorate. Brush on the rest of the egg and bake in a moderate oven.

Babootee

1 cup left-over cold meat (any mixture)
1/2 teaspoon minced red pepper
1 medium chopped onion
1 slice stale bread
1 egg
salt to taste
2 teaspoons butter
milk to moisten
1 dessertspoon curry powder
breadcrumbs

Mince the cold meat, add the seasonings, chopped onion, 1 teaspoon butter and the curry powder. Beat the egg and mix with the meat mixture. Soak the slice of bread in cold water, squeeze dry, shred finely and add it with a little salt to taste, and some milk to moisten the mixture. Grease a small casserole with a bit of butter, put the mixture in, sprinkle the top lightly with breadcrumbs and dot with the rest of butter. Bake this uncovered at 180°C, 350°F or Gas 4 until lightly browned. Serve as a supper dish.

Sopped Biscuits

This is an old recipe. A round hard biscuit was originally used but Eclipse biscuits must be substituted now. Long ago it was a favourite among some mothers, who gave it to their children around 9.00 a.m. School used to begin at 10 a.m. Lunch was usually a cake or sandwich and fruit. The child's main meal was taken at 4.00 or 5.00 p.m. in the afternoon as there were fewer after school activities. Recipe to serve 4-6

16 single Eclipse biscuits
4oz Salt fish (desalted by soaking in cold water - may be done overnight)
8oz of salt meat (desalted in boiling water and refrigerated)
1 medium sized carrot thinly sliced
1 small onion chopped and few sprigs of green herbs
1 teaspoon dried herbs
1/4 teaspoon black or white pepper
1 tablespoon cooking butter
1 cup green peas (optional)
Water

Cover biscuits with cold water and add a little salt. When soft crush with a fork, keeping moist. Cook sliced carrots and green peas in saucepan with onion and herbs. Add fish, meat and biscuits and mix together over low heat. Stir well together. Do not over cook. Serve hot with butter or left over gravy.

Rita Springer's Caribbean Cookbook

Glossary

Chocho — A member of the melon family which is also known as cristophene. It is a green pear-shaped fruit used as a vegetable.

Coco — Also known as Eddo. A small round starchy root vegetable, brown-skinned and hariy, with white flesh.

Coconut Cream — Coconut milk.

Conch — A shell fish of the mollusc family. It lives in a large spiral shell and may be a variety of sizes.

Conkies Paimies — (see page 133 and 135).

Conquintay — The creole name for plantain flolur which is made from just under-ripe plantains. They are sliced, allowed to dry thoroughly in the sun or oven and then ground into flour. The flour, which is used for making porridge, is now factory processed in Guyana.

Dasheen — A large root tuber with a dark brown rough skin. The flesh is dark, and when cooked, is not quite as tasty as other root vegetables.

Eddo — See Coco.

Egg Plant — A dark-skinned fleshy vegetable also known as melongene, bolangere, garden egg, or aubergine.

Escallion — Spring onions or chives.
Eschalot — Another name for Escallion.

Foo-foo — Pounded plantain.

Granadilla — The large fruit of a climbing plant. It is pale green, resembles a melon and grows from 1-10in. in length. The flesh has a delicious, slightly acid, flavour and is chiefly used for making drinks and ices. It is also called Barbadine.

Groundnut — Peanut.

Ground Provisions — All starchy root vegetables.

Jira — The small dry spicy seeds from a sweet herb, used in making Roti and in other Indian dishes.

Mango — A tropical fruit with thick skin, yellow flesh which is firm and sweet, and a flat hairy seed. There are many varieties. It is available tinned in many countries.

Mauby — A drink made frm the bark of a tree which grows in some areas of the Caribbean. The bark is dried and sold in pieces and is very bitter. It is boiled with spices and sugar and made into a syrup which is added, in small quantities, to water, sweetened to taste, iced, swizzled and served as Mauby Drink, see page 117.

Molasses — Cane syrup.
Okra — Also called ochroes or 'ladies' fingers'. They are finger-length green ribbed and hairy pods which grow profusely. They are best when picked young and freshly boiled. They are also used in the dish cou-cou, see page 131.

Otaheite apple Also known as pomerac, plum rose and molly apple, this is a pear-shaped red fruit with white flesh. It grows to about 3-4 inches in length and is used chiefly for stewing and making jam.

Paw paw A large round or oblong melon-like fruit which grows from its tree trunk between umbrella-shaped leaves. The thick yellow juicy flesh has a delicious flavour and there are numerous black seeds in the centre of the fruit. The green paw paw is sometimes used as a vegetable, also as a preserve. It is also called papaya.

Black eye peas Tropical white peas with a black patch which grow in long pods. The dried peas are available in many countries.

Congo peas Green, pigeon or gunga peas.

Channa peas Also known as Chick peas, they resemble dried whole peas but are slightly larger. They are chiefly used in Indian cookery.

Gunga peas Tropical green peas, also dried and available in many countries. Sometimes called Congo peas.

Pepper Pot A very hot meat stew with cassareep, see page 137.

Plantains A member of the banana family. The large fruits are not eaten raw but cooked when ripe. They are also cooked when green or under-ripe, especially in the preparation of the dish 'foo-foo'.

Red peas The Caribbean name for red beans.

Shaddock A member of the citrus family which resembles a grapefruit but is much larger, and the frlesh is sometimes pink in colour. It is used as fruit and the skin and pith are made into a preserve.

Soursop A large dark green heart-shaped fruit with spiny rough skin. The pithy flesh is slightly acid and juicy with black seeds. It is very popular when made into punch or ice-cream because of its refreshing flavour.

Tamarind The fruit of a very large tree, it is a brown pod about 3-4 inches long which grows in bunches. When ripe the pods may be cracked easily to reveal black seeds covered with brown puop which is used in making some condiments. The seeds may also be steeped in cane syrup for several months to preserve them.

Tannia A tuberous root, similar to eddoes but larger, used as a vegetable.

Index

156

Eggs, Fried, and Bacon 63
  Scrambled 63
  Stuffed 121

F
Filling, Sardine and Egg 121
  Tomato-cheese 121
Fish, Baked and Stuffed 33
  Pie 33
  Soup 25
  and Vegetable Mould 33
Floating Island 83
Flying Fish, 41
  Fried 35
  Steamed 35
Fowl Down-in-Rice 133
French Dressing 21
Fresh Fish vs Iced Fish 39
Fried, Cabbage 73
  Eggs & Bacon 63
  Flying Fish 35
  Rice 139
Fritters, Cornmeal 77
  Pineapple 77
Frizzled Salt Fish 37
Frosting, Fluffy 99
Fruit Cake, Rich 107
Fruit Punch, Mixed 118
Fruit Salad, Fresh 83
Fudge, Chocolate 113

G
Garlic Pork 137
Gelatine Desserts - Guava Whip 85
Ginger, Beer 117
  Bread 103
  Squares 111
Glacé Icing 99
Goat, Curried 53
Grapefruit Baskets, or Orange 83

Gravy, Brown 47
Green Corn Dumplings 129
Grill, Mixed 51
Grilled, Pork Chops 51
Guava, Cheese 113
  Drink 117
  Ice Cream 87
  Jelly 111
  Whip 85

H
Ham, Baked 49
  Picnic Shoulder of 49
Hard Sauce 89
Hot Pot 54

I
Ice, Coconut 113
Ice-Cream, Coconut 87
  Guava 87
  Vanilla 87
Iced Tea 118
Icing, Glacé 99

J
Jam, or Swiss Roll 101
  Pineapple 111
  Tarts 93
Jelly, Guava 111
Jerk Pork 129
Jug-Jug 133

K
Kedgeree 35

L
Lamb, Curried 53
Lemonade 117
Lemon Meringue Pie 93

M

Macaroni, Cheese 61
  with Vegetables and Mince 55
Mango, Brown Betty 89
  Chutney 21
  Cream Mould 85
  Drink 117
Marble Cake 101
Marinade, Basic for meats 19
Marmalade, Orange or Tangerine 111
Marzipan 107
Mauby 117
Meat Patties 125
Mince Pies 107
Mixed Fruit Punch 118
Mixed Grill 51
Mixed Vegetable Soup 27
Mock Apple Sauce 47
Moulded Vegetable Salad 75
Mustard Sauce 59
Mutton, Curried 53
  Soup 26

O
Okra Soup 27
Omelette, Vegetable 63
Orange Marmalade, or Tangerine 111
Orange Trifle, or Pineapple 85

P
Paella 143
Paimie 135
Pancake, Batter 91, 139
  Rolls 139
Parsley Sauce 59
Pastelles 143
Pastry, Rich Short Crust 125
Patties, Meat 125
Pawpaw Water Ice 87
Peanut Brittle 111
Peas, Doved 78
Pigeon Pea Stew 54

Pigeon Peas & Rice 69
Pepper Pot 137
  Soup 129
Pie, Lemon Meringue 93
  Mince 107
  Pumpkin 92
  Shepherd's 145
Pineapple, Fritters 77
  Jam 111
  or Orange Trifle 85
Pone, Cassava 137
  Cornmeal 103
Pork, Baked 47
  Chops, Grilled 51
  Garlic 137
  Jerk 129
  Shoulder, Stuffed 47
  Sweet and Sour 141
Potato & Shrimp Casserole 55
Press Cookies 123
Pudding, Raisin Bread 89
  and Souse 131
  Split Pea 79
  Vanilla 89
Pumpkin, Pie 92
  Soup 25
Punch a Créme 119
Punch, Mixed Fruit 118
  Rum (Cold) 119

R
Rabbit Soup, or Chicken 25
Raisin, Buns or Bun Bread 105
  Bread 104
  Bread Pudding 89
Rice, and Callaloo 55
  Calypso 78
  Cook-up 54
  Fowl-down-in 133
  Fried 139
  and Peas (Jamaican) 129

Spanish 143
Rich Short Crust Pastry 125
Rich Fruit Cake 107
Rock Buns 97
Rolls, Dinner 105
  Jam or Swiss 101
  Pancake 139
Roti 141
Rum Punch (cold) 119
  Sauce 89

S
Salad, Bok Choy 73
  Cucumber and Avocado 75
  Fresh Fruit 83
  Green, Tossed 75
  Moulded Vegetable 75
Salt Fish, and Ackee 129
  Cakes 39
  Cakes, Curried 123
  Frizzled 37
  and Melongenes 39
Sandwiches 121
Sardine and Egg Filling 121
Sauce, Cheese 59
  Cocktail 123
  Cream or White 59
  Economical Custard 89
  Hard 89
  Parsley 59
  Rum 89
Scalloped Sweet Potato & Onions 67
Scones, (Basic Recipe) 97
Scorpion 118
Scrambled Eggs 63
Sea Eggs 41
Seasoned Flour 19
Seasoning Mixture 21
Shepherd's Pie 145

Sherbet, Pineapple, Tangerine, Lime or Orange 87
Shrimp & Potato Casserole 55
Shrimp, Curried 37
Skirt Soup 26
Sopped Biscuits 145
Sorrel (1), & (2) 118
Soup, Beef with Vegetables 27
  Breadfruit 26
  Callaloo 27
  Chilled Cucumber 25
  Eddoe 26
  Fish 25
  Mixed Vegetable 27
  Mutton 26
  Okra 27
  Pumpkin 25
  Rabbit or Chicken 25
  Skirt 26
  Split Pea 26
Spanish Rice 143
Special Rum Punch 119
Spinach, and Corn Salmagundi 79
  Cakes 77
Split Pea Pudding 79
  Soup 26
Steak, Barbecued 45
Stew, Beef and Vegetables 45
Stewed Chicken 53
Stir Fry, Vegetables 73
Stuffed, Eggs 121
  Sweet Peppers 73
Sugar Cake, Coconut 113
Sweet and Sour Pork 141
Sweet Peppers, Stuffed 73
Sweet Potato, Caramel 67
  and Onions, Scalloped 67

T
Tamarind Drink 117

Index

158

Tangerine or Orange Marmalade 111
Tarts, Coconut Custard 93
　Jam 93
Tea, Iced 118
　Ring 92
Tips for Making Pastry 125
Tomato-Cheese Filling 121
Tossed Green Salad 75
Trifle, Orange or Pineapple 85
Two-egg Cake 97

V
Vegetable, Omelette 63
Vegetable, Stir Fry 73
　Salad, Moulded 75

W
Waffles 91
White Bread 104
Whole-wheat Bread 104